Something About
the BLUES

an unlikely collection of poetry

AL YOUNG

**sourcebooks
mediaFusion**

An Imprint of
Sourcebooks Inc. ®
Naperville, Illinois

Published by Sourcebooks MediaFusion, an imprint of Sourcebooks, Inc.
P.O. Box 4410, Naperville, Illinois 60567-4410
(630) 961-3900
Fax: (630) 961-2168
www.sourcebooks.com

Audio selections were variously recorded and produced by:

• Jym Marks at Nicole Studios; Fremont, CA in June 2004
• InnerSpark Summer Arts Program at CalArts (California Institute of the Arts), Santa Clarita, CA (Al Young in live performance with the Ralph Jones Quartet: Ralph Jones: tenor saxophone and woodwinds, Kenn Cox, piano; Edwin Livingston, bass; Harris Eisenstadt, drums) in July 2006
• Tom Bruce and Marc Silber at Grizzly Peak Studios; Berkeley, CA in July 2007

Library of Congress Cataloging-in-Publication Data

Young, Al
   Something about the blues / Al Young.
      p. cm.
   "Includes an audio CD with Al Young's dynamic, soulful readings of more than 20 of the poems from the book"—From the publisher.
   1. Blues (Music)—Poetry. I. Title.
   PS3575.O683S57 2007
   811'.54—dc22
                                        2007036614

Printed and bound in the United States of America.
IN 10 9 8 7 6 5 4 3 2 1

For Michael Young,
my beloved son

Acknowledgments

Not all but some of these poems, many in slightly different form, previously appeared in the following publications: *Alaska Quarterly Review* (Peggy Shumaker), *Aldebaran Review* (John Oliver Simon), *Asili: The Journal of Multicultural HeartSpeak* (Joseph P. McNair), *Brilliant Corners: A Journal of Literature & Jazz* (Sascha Feinstein), *Counter/Measures* (X. J. Kennedy), *Crystalline Flight* (Heidi Spitzer-Chang), *Konch* (Ishmael Reed), *New York Review of Books*/Antaeus Selection (Daniel Halpern), *nocturnes (re) view* (Giovanni Singleton), *Haight Ashbury Literary Journal* (Conyus Calhoun, Indigo Hotchkiss, Alice Rogoff), *Hambone* (Nathaniel Mackey), *Marin Poetry Center Anthology* (Cathy Shea), *Paris Review* (Michael Benedikt, George Plimpton), *Reed: A Journal of Poetry & Place* (Jeanette Maldonado), *Ploughshares* (Jane Hirshfield), *River City* (Gordon Osing), *San Diego Reader* (Judith Pinch), *Seattle Review* (Colleen J. McElroy), *Yardbird Reader* (Ishmael Reed and Al Young); *Heaven: Poems 1956–1990*, *The Blues Don't Change: New & Selected Poems*, *The Sound of Dreams Remembered: Poems: 1990–2000*, *Coastal Nights and Inland Afternoons: Poems 2001–2006*, *Kinds of Blue: Musical Memoirs*, *The Colors of Nature: Culture, Identity and the Natural World* (Alison Hawthorne Deming and Lauret E. Savoy, editors), *Oakland Out Loud: Poetry and Prose in Celebration of "There"* (Karla Brundage and Kim Shuck).

Books by Al Young

Dancing (poems)

Snakes (novel)

The Song Turning Back into Itself (poetry)

Who Is Angelina? (novel)

Geography of the Near Past (poems)

Sitting Pretty (novel)

Ask Me Now (novel)

Bodies & Soul (musical memoir)

The Blues Don't Change: New and Selected Poems (poetry)

Kinds of Blue (musical memoirs)

Yardbird Lives! (anthology) coedited with with Ishmael Reed

Things Ain't What They Used to Be (poetry)

Seduction By Light (novel)

Mingus Mingus: Two Memoirs (with Janet Coleman)

Heaven: Collected Poems 1956–1990

Straight No Chaser (poetry chapbook)

Drowning in the Sea of Love (musical memoirs)

African American Literature: A Brief Introduction and Anthology (textbook)

Conjugal Visits (poetry chapbook)

The Literature of California (anthology) with Jack Hicks, James D. Houston, and Maxine Hong Kingston

The Sound of Dreams Remembered: Poems 1990–2000

Coastal Nights and Inland Afternoons: Poems 2001–2006

Contents

*CD Contents

1 The Weary Blues (by Langston Hughes)

2 Dawn at Oakland Airport

3 A Poem for Listeners

4 April in Paris

5 Elevator Over the Hill

6 Sundays in Democracies

7 Animal

8 A Low-Flying Blues for Somebody

9 Blue Monday

10 Lost Passport Blues

11 Distances

12 Giving the Drummer Some

13 Saudades: The Portuguese Blues

14 *Introduction to* My Spanish Heart

15 My Spanish Heart

16 Clearing the Way for Ecstasy

17 Straight No Chaser

18 Conjugal Visits

19 Los Angeles, Los Angeles: One Long-Shot, One Cutaway

20 Rush

21 The James Cotton Band at Keystone

22 Squirrels

23 The Buddhist Way Out West Reflects on Boots

24 Doo-wop: The Moves

25 Tribute

26 Romance without Finance

Epigraph

Sky blue, ocean blue, lake blue, ice blue, blood blue, vein blue, neon blue, flame blue, periwinkle blue, steely blue, nipple blue, royal blue, true blue, moon blue, midnight blue, mountain blue, snow blue, powder blue, algae blue, devil blue, heavenly blue, blossom blue, Nile blue, stocking blue, moldy blue, radiant blue, electric blue, shadow blue, twilight blue, navy blue, star blue, movie blue, misty blue, ribbon blue, fox blue, feather blue, eye blue, thigh blue, grass blue, jazz blue, and on and on into the blueness of your very essence—not to even mention exclusively human kinds of blue.

Introduction:
Something About the Blues

Beaded and threaded throughout America's musical mosaic, the blues make you feel and hear. Sometimes you can count them off in measures and beats, but largely they dwell in a feral state; blues truth is wild and menacing.

Like poetry, the blues will always be dramatically unpredictable, sometimes torturous and sometimes pleasurable. Ever resistant to classroom analysis or the glacial and invasive systems of calculus, the blues stay new. Without passport or visa, the blues remain ubiquitous; they sneak and snake, worm, winnow, Bogart and charm their way across all borders and bypasses.

Whether you're listening to Robert Johnson, Memphis Minnie, Jelly Roll Morton, Louis Armstrong, Bessie Smith, Sophie Tucker, Ethel Waters, Muddy Waters, Duke Ellington, Count Basie, Woody Herman, Mary Lou Williams, George Gershwin, Johnny Mercer, Nat King Cole, Hank Williams, Thelonious Monk, Sonny Terry & Brownie McGee, Billie Holiday, Frank Sinatra, Chet Atkins, the Ravens, the Orioles, the Crows, the Flamingos, Little Anthony and the Imperials, Marvin Gaye, Aretha Franklin, Big Mama Thornton, Elvis Presley, Miles Davis, Bill Evans, Willie Nelson, Howlin' Wolf, Barry White, Charlie Parker, Bud Powell, Manhattan Transfer, Bobbie Gentry, the Beach Boys, Ray Charles, Johnny Hartman, Stan Getz, Ella Fitzgerald, Jimmy Smith, the Neville Brothers, Odetta, Charles Mingus, Weather Report, Bonnie Raitt, Katy Webster, James Brown, Earl Scruggs & Lester Flatt, the whole Marsalis family, Donna Summers, Buck Owens, John Coltrane, Ry Cooder, Taj Mahal, Dizzy Gillespie, Little Walter, Little Brother Montgomery, Robert Johnson,

Charlie Mariano, Esther Phillips, Slim Harpo, Jimmy Reed or Leonard Bernstein—you're listening to the blues.

The irreducible radical of music, the blues defy and accommodate all takers and givers; that is, all listeners and dancers, all players and singers. There's plenty to be said about a nation that has given our world the blues; a national culture whose signature tonality continues to be the blues. All combined, these wayward pages say something about the blues.

As early as 1947—in a second-grade classroom at the Kingston Elementary School for Colored in Laurel, Mississippi—Miz Chapman, my tireless and inspired all-day second-grade teacher, was smuggling down to me the majesty and magic of poetry and blues. An unrepentant and dogmatic Afro-Christian, who regarded the blues as devilish, Miz Chapman nevertheless forced us to memorize poems, especially works by colored writers.

The class day began with us singing "Lift Every Voice and Sing" (sometimes called The Negro National Anthem), which seguéd into "The Star-Spangled Banner." Later in the day—as we moved from writing, arithmetic, manners, history, geography, hygiene, music and literature—we pupils stood in front of the class to recite the stuff we'd memorized. I can never forget the wound the poem's sound delivered:

> *The singer stopped playing and went to bed*
> *While the Weary Blues echoed through his head.*
> *He slept like a rock or a man that's dead.*

Just as Ida Cox's classic song reminds us that "Wild Women Don't Have the Blues," so these pages, I hope, will remind the world that dead men don't sing.

The Weary Blues

by Langston Hughes

Droning a drowsy syncopated tune,
Rocking back and forth to a mellow croon,
    I heard a Negro play.
Down on Lenox Avenue the other night
By the pale dull pallor of an old gas light
    He did a lazy sway . . .
    He did a lazy sway . . .
To the tune o' those Weary Blues.
With his ebony hands on each ivory key
He made that poor piano moan with melody.
    O Blues!
Swaying to and fro on his rickety stool
He played that sad raggy tune like a musical fool.
    Sweet Blues!
Coming from a black man's soul.
    O Blues!
In a deep song voice with a melancholy tone
I hear that Negro sing, that old piano moan—

"Ain't got nobody in all this world,
    Ain't got nobody but ma self.
    I's gwine to quit ma frownin'
    And put ma troubles on the shelf."

Thump, thump, thump, went his foot on the floor.
He played a few chords then he sang some more—
    "I got the Weary Blues
        And I can't be satisfied.
        Got the Weary Blues
        And can't be satisfied—
        I ain't happy no mo'
        And I wish that I had died."
And far into the night he crooned that tune.
The stars went out and so did the moon.
The singer stopped playing and went to bed
While the Weary Blues echoed through his head.
He slept like a rock or a man that's dead.

Dawn at Oakland Airport

TRACK 2

Aggression keeps arriving but almost never departs.
As quiet as it's kept, greed bops along for the ride.
Do you need James Brown hollering in your ear
at 6 a.m. when you've gotten all of two hours sleep,
misread your itinerary and coldly missed the flight?
I can't stand it, either, James. The Godfather of Soul
and all the other Godfathers share a mission this morning,
and that's to put another hit on peace and quietude.
You don't need no Johnny Cash, no saxophone quartet
version of the Temptations' "My Girl," no "Goldfinger,"
no "Ring of Fire," no Earth, Wind & Fire doing "Hearts
Afire," no jaunty disco deco from the decadent Seventies.
What you need is Z's and more Z's—Zambia, Zanzibar,
Zihuatanejo, no, Canal Zone, Zone 51, UFO's, out of here,
out of ear shot surely. And when two advancing armies
in the war on silence conjoin, when the foreground music
of Gate 10 crisses across Gate 8's background music,
you know no zone can ever be demilitarized again.
Green, brown, the hills that ring this East Bay underdog
airport can't compete, and sky—O lazy, hazy sky of summer,
what brings you here in April?—the sky is battling, too.

Give us Slim Harpo: "The sky is crying / Look at the tears
roll down the street." Give us liberty to chose your death.
The breath you hold whispers the unspeakable:
"Can things actually get any worse?" Yes, saith Phoenix,
yes, saith Las Vegas, Los Angeles saith yes, and Houston agrees.
By the time you get to Newark, maybe *The Sopranos* and
all the electric pianos in the world will have gone on break.

A Poem for Listeners

TRACK 3

If, uplifting those fanning ears, the elephant
can hear ultra high frequency mating
calls placed from miles beyond this deafening sky,
then why can't sultry laughter like yours—
all piquancy and sass—take off? The rumble of it
sometimes makes its way to parts of me I long
to tour but haven't. In shining ring within ring,
the satellite brightness of your laughter lights heaven
at hand, out-circling itself like a rock dropped into a pond.
If Ravi Shankar could hear the gouache of anguish

7

washing through St. Coltrane's cries, or if Ravel could hear
the Gypsy strains of Spain that ruffled his composure
a borderline away, or if bats can hear the sound
of fruit flies walking, and if every city makes and leaves
its own soundprint, then, tell me, with your next hard laugh,
what animal ancestor of ours flowered in the sound of the note
the chord never needs to round itself out, but takes in
—thankful. Unpack, relax, and I'll tell you another one.

Love Listening to Lionel Hampton Play the Vibraharp

Making love listening to Lionel Hampton play,
every lick counts, every quiver socks in and registers.
Adding it up, you push yourself on me and I accept
every morsel with a sigh. In this undulant performance
clichés don't stand a chance. Your heart, as raw as sand,
leaks into every pore love opens up, as if, as if, as if,
as though this might be the last time we can dock

and beach each other in perfectly legal splendor.
O how they jibe, these late at night and sultry vibes.
The walking, the living dream has nothing on
the you who moves naked through our minds.
Please, don't explain. I wasn't there in Spain with you,
but, don't forget I, too, know the kind of home
you make in Rome. And who could blame him,
that smart señor, his savvy lust, his taste for tourist goods?
In this resonant moment, Hamp is heaping it on,
"picking 'em up and laying them down," he'd say.
And you are every chorus, every bridge, every intro
I've ever memorized or faked. And still somehow
it all spills out, a rush; it all pours out original.
It's OK that you can't dance; I can't, either.
We know the steps, though, don't we?—the dips,
the moves, the gracious, out-of-fashion guanguanco—
so when we drag and drop all pretense, passion sounds.

Ars Poetica

All that we did was human,
stupid, easily forgiven,
Not quite right.
Gary Snyder

Now that nothing has worked out
and the beautiful trees
are again in winter, feeding
on lean November light; the world,
like the cold, tentative yet tight
around his skin, his heart about
to pound right out of him,
he can linger on this corner again,
unnoticed, another dude in another street,
waiting for someone to keep an appointment
in the frozen belly of a large city,
no string quartets, no studio brass
bands to grace the meaningless background,
only the warmth of personal sun,
a blossoming peace stretching out.
In the soft folds of his brain—
she arrives as in a living photograph,

her everyday breath steaming the air,
warm under coat and sweater, simple
skirt, boots, the colored elastic of
her pants underneath snapped snugly
into place at the waist, at the thigh.

You Catch Yourself on a Train with Yo-Yo Ma

for Kari Winter

You catch yourself on a train with Yo-Yo Ma.
Dapper sucker that he is, Yo-Yo's got his cello
all packed in advance and as always he is dressed
if not to the nines, then certainly to the sevens
and eights. You can feel all the Bach, all the Beethoven,
all the jazz and tango and Kalahari bush people
pouring out of him; all the beauty and sadness
he has spent his whole life attending and exploring.

Suddenly you hear yourself say, "Hey, Yo, on TV,
well—actually it was in the backseat of your friends'
car where their toddler was strapped—all the way
from Vermont to Quebec you heard this soundtrack,
a kid show, where some kid stepped up to him, Yo,
and then just grinned and blushed. It took another character
to roll it out for the dumb toddler: 'It isn't Yo Mama,
it's Yo-Yo Ma.' But it didn't matter. By the time
you got to play whatever they'd arranged, you'd scored."
When I asked why you, the great cellist, were riding
a train, you smiled and said, "This is Japan, my man.
Not only do the fast trains work and run on time;
they separate and segregate into cell phone cars and
no cell phones allowed like you have smoking and no smoking
in the States. Even a cellist needs a cell phone now and again.
But on a journey like this, I need silence and solitude."
You got it, you get it. You sit way back and shut the hell up.

12

April in Paris

TRACK 4

after Yip Harburg & Vernon Duke

It was here in that one-time, one-stop, lighted blue
of Paris at ease, close to the Cluny, in splendid,
straight-up noontime shadow that your slow and
measuring eyes met more than their burning match.

The smooth warmth of your whisper along my neck,
the nappy back of it, where you'd peeled back
its soft, excited collar to tell me everything you'd learned
or discerned in a city where love and prices flirt.

A product of standstill winters, sudden summers, sultry
prejudice, and heartland steak-and-whiskey afternoons,
you'd blown in from the States, an orphan of the arts—
Mary Cassatt, Josephine Baker, Mary Lou Williams,

Jean Seberg. What breathlessness overtakes me here?
Brushing and combing out memories of your touch,
in a season as uncertain as coastal fog moving inland
from the loveless edges of that country we'd both fled,

I shiver. Whom could we run to if not one another?
Back home we knew what it was like to be the other—
displaced, despised, imprisonable. We watched and fought.
The colors of loss deepened. Yearning to break free,

unconsciously American, we counted our chickens, certain
that the ships we'd always banked on would sail in.
In Paris, our adopted country of each other's arms,
whose borders blurred all time, all common market sense,

we saved the slow but steady squeeze of night, of time;
the way it smothered darkness, the way it mothered light.
The April of your frightened French was like that, too;
you had no words for holiday tables, for chestnuts in bloom.

Parisian light, like light at home—Detroit, Des Moines—
lit up your waifish eyes. I said, "Think twice before you speak."
Over here you mostly knew the blues; *rue* rhymed with blue.
There couldn't be too much light, or too much touch.

Elevator Over the Hill

TRACK 5

after Carla Bley

That was one evil elevator,
had a mind of its own.
It took you where it wanted
and brought you back
when it felt like it.
This elevator went in for trying
to crush people in its doors,
and woe unto the unwary passenger
who stuck an arm out to stop it.

This elevator would just as soon snap
a limb just like—like you would
a popsicle stick. If you pressed 10,
it stopped at 2, 3, 6 and
stuck at 7. Or if for some reason
it whisked you all the way
to the floor of your desire,

the door wouldn't open. You could ring
the alarm but no one would ever be there to help.

This elevator reeked continuously
of strong disinfectant, unpleasant perfumes
and colognes, take-away fast food, garbage
and farts, illicit cigars and even reefer some nights.
Sometimes you suspected it of substance abuse.

This elevator was a bring-down; it had a strong will.
It must've been, it had to be over the hill.

Landscape Mode

Overlooking the Cumberland River,
Clarksville, Tennessee,
early November 1996

In ancient Chinese paintings we see more sky than
earth, so when clouds hurry by in silver-gray
inkbursts of rolling readiness right along the river,

ripe with rain, rushing the road of time along,
pushing back light, belittling the black and white clarity
of Hollywood in its prime, the eye climbs down to greet

with shining gusto trees along the shore. Opryland
beyond the frame, the blue horizon hidden in a sea
of possibilities. And beyond this there's jazz: Jimmy Giuffre's

"Train on the River" stretched out strong like a pet cat
—and that's that. But not quite. This poem paints
poorly what sketchers and colorists do best. The rest

should come out empty, allowing you to fill in your own
basic emptiness, your openness, your self-portrait
forged and catalogued; on quiet exhibit, on temporary loan.

Descended from clouds immensely more ancient than China,
you never quit becoming the background, the field in a sky
whose subtle earthiness sails over our heads altogether.

Just Gimme Some Kinda Sign, Girl

The Follies Burlesk Theater,
San Francisco, 1970

Tell me now, was it the girl, or was it the world?

While the midnight hour was ripening in bloom,

she barefooted her smiling way out onto the stage.

Do step-folks count? She could've been your step-

granddaughter from some deadened love-nerve;

it could've been your daughter you were oo-ogling.

Traffic smacked on at 16th and Mission, your face

a sorry San Francisco witness in midst of it.

Stripper: one who takes off garments for payment

one hush at a time to the thrill and yell of driven men.

Life gushes through this girl the way the will to procreate

presses her watchers. "Just gimme some kinda sign, girl."

That's all the singer asks. "Show me that you're mine, girl."
Tease, she's picked Brenton Wood to sing and sign her in.
Her moves make grown men moan and women whimper.

This is when midnight kicks in—at this night-kissed moment.
Baring a shoulder, a back, breast, a belly, some thighs, some
leg, some butt, and finally some coochie, hey, wha'choo

gonna do, wha'choo gonna say? "The night is like a melody,
beware, my foolish heart"? Somebody already wrote that;
somebody, plenty bodies, already done this bump-and-grind.

So what's the point? What is it these poems keep driving at?
What geographies, what states—if you please—keep you
aroused and on the edge of your seat to hear and see love

acted out again and again as if there'd never been another you?
It was always the ways she moved to it, wasn't it?
It wasn't at all about the music—or was it, was it, was it?

The Blues Don't Change

"Now I'll tell you about the Blues.
All Negroes like Blues. Why?
Because they was born with the Blues.
And now everybody have the Blues.
Sometimes they don't know what it is."
Leadbelly

And I was born with you, wasn't I, Blues?
Wombed with you, wounded, reared and forwarded
from address to address, stamped, stomped
and returned to sender by nobody else but you,
Blue Rider, writing me off every chance you
got, you mean old grudgeful-hearted, table-
turning demon, you, you sexy soul-sucking gem.

Blue diamond in the rough, you *are* forever.
You can't be outfoxed don't care how they cut
and smuggle and shine you on, you're like a
shadow, too dumb and stubborn and necessary
to let them turn you into what you ain't
with color or theory or powder or paint.

That's how you can stay in style without sticking
and not getting stuck. You know how to sting
where I can't scratch, and you move from frying
pan to skillet the same way you move people
to go to wiggling their bodies, juggling their
limbs, loosening that goose, upping their voices,
opening their pores, rolling their hips and lips.

They can shake their boodies but they can't shake *you*.

The Elvis I Knew Well Was Spiritual

The Elvis I knew well was spiritual.
The books he'd read on mystics, yoga, Jung
and Jesus, Buddha—long before your digital
technology kicked in and Mao Tse-Tung
became an icon you could click—he tried
to buy enlightenment. He thought a check

21

might do the trick: big bucks, love-tendered, wide
and blank. No deal. No Ouija board, no deck
of tarot cards could trump his fate. His star
beamed underneath (or far beyond) the God
he knew as blackness, gospel, blues. As far
as light-years went, Elvis could ride and nod.
He couldn't get high on glory, glamour, fame.
Blissless, he drugged you with his moves, his name.

A Dance for Ma Rainey

I'm going to be just like you, Ma
Rainey this monday morning
clouds puffing up out of my head
like those balloons
that float above the faces of white people
in the funnypapers

I'm going to hover in the corners
of the world, Ma
& sing from the bottom of hell

22

up to the tops of high heaven
& send out scratchless waves of yellow
& brown & that basic black honey
misery

I'm going to cry so sweet
& so low
 & so dangerous,
Ma,
that the message is going to reach you
back in 1922
where you shimmer
snaggle-toothed
perfumed &
powdered
in your bauble beads

hair pressed & tied back
throbbing with that sick pain
I know
& hide so well
that pain that blues
jives the world with
aching to be heard
that downness
that bottomlessness

23

first felt by some stolen delta nigger
swamped under with redblooded american agony;
reduced to the sheer shit
of existence
that bred
& battered us all,
Ma,
the beautiful people
our beautiful brave black people
who no longer need to jazz
or sing to themselves in murderous vibrations
or play the veins of their strong tender arms
with needles
to prove we're still here

24

Blues My Naughty Poetry Taught Me

1/

How much of you was raised in jazz-fed otherness?

And how much did Thelonious Monk and loneliness

compose you like a thoughtful bass solo melting on ears

that shone when they listened to the world slowed down

in chromatic tones so inviting you sometimes wonder—

the childhood you spent dreaming to drummers dreaming.

2/

In a country so contrary

with nobody on drums, just

a drum machine, can you dance

with any sincerity, much less

to Otis Redding's "Security"?

Who's on bass? Anybody home?

Does anybody ever get to first?

How does a kiss get you anywhere?

25

3/

In parking lots our kisses counted big.
You knew the scores, you kept me up.

4/

When blue songs drift aloft, there's no telling where anything is going. UK
accents turn North American, Nigerian Delta thoughts get versed in oil. To ask
that you be touched with love is all that ever matters.

If you'd ever played Beth Orton's oddly bluesy "Touch Me with Your Love" for
Miles Davis, he would've made her a million dollars. As it was, he recorded
"Time After Time" and made a whole lot of money for Cyndi Lauper. Miles had
an ear for young women like Lauper, Laura Nyro and others who wrote and
phrased with feeling.

5/

Mind games and thoughts of time differed
in the 18th, 19th, 20th Centuries, when space
was open like wounds and minds were razored.

Hot lost trails of consciousness, windows,

winter, what star do you think you are?

French clouds, French blue, language gauges this:

your swiftest kiss—jellyfish pink, squid-ink sweet.

Sea-fences, industrial washed-ups, slushy tracks

and rickety light: skies so soulfully watercolored

you'd have to be an arts commissioner not to see it.

Seen across the Bay through trees and the undersides

of freeways San Francisco looks lonely at the end

of one bridge and the beginning of another. Rainy train

gray Amtrak's got me funneling poetry, channeling prose.

Poetry and blues and jazz, you've handed me the key

to every heart you ever captured or held spellbound.

27

The Prestidigitator 1

What you gonna do when they burn your barrelhouse down?
What you gonna do when they burn your barrelhouse down?
Gonna move out the piano & barrelhouse on the ground.
traditional Afro-American blues

A prestidigitator makes things disappear,
vanish, not unlike a well-paid bookkeeper
or tax consultant or champion consumer

The poet is a prestidigitator, he makes
our old skins disappear & re-clothes you

in sturdy raiment of thought, feeling, soul,
dream & happenstance. Consider him villain of
the earthbound, a two-fisted cowboy with
pencil in one hand & eraser in the other

dotting the horizon of your heart with cool
imaginary trees but rubbing out more than he
leaves in for space so light can get thru

The Prestidigitator 2

I draw hats on rabbits, sew women back
together, let fly from my pockets flocks of
vibratory hummingbirds. The things I've got

up my sleeve would activate the most listless
of landscapes (the cracked-earth heart of a bigot,
say) with pigeons that boogaloo, with flags that

light up stabbed into the brain. Most of all it's
enslaving mumbo-jumbo that I'd wipe away, a trick
done by walking thru mirrors to the other side

Michigan Water (or, How Lake Superior Informs Us)

Shining, the silver-gray glow of Lake Superior informs
us slowly all day, all night, all year, all century long.
Those dark-blooded Blue Note jazz dreams a poet soon has
in the Upper Peninsula originate in Upper not Lower Egypt.
Upper Michigan and Lower Michigan, the Rabbit forever
hippity-hopping above the Glove, seem to share nothing
with Ra, the ancient god of sun and sacrifice—at first.
Yet on any uncloudy day, Marquette, Escanaba, Manistee,
Sault Sainte Marie, Menominee flee the pent-up heat
of iced, palatial dreams. Light, like water, sees and saws
through mind and stone alike. Swishing whitefish, too, wish
upon waves of thought sunlight supplies, and then supports.
Walking such lake waters, Jesus might utter: "It is my Father
who doeth the works. You can do likewise, and more besides."
Blinded by the gleam of this vision, an upper, a sleeper thaws.
Stilled again with wonder, and seasoned with hardship,
seasoned with love, we stand informed—and thickly warmed.

Ba-lues Done Gone Ballistic

"Ba-lue Bolivar Bal-lues-are" is Thelonious Monk's title for the slow 12-bar blues he composed for his close friend the Baroness Pannonica de Koenigswarter when she resided at Manhattan's Hotel Bolivar in the late 1950s. The blues link the DNA of all of America's music.

Ba-lues (as in red-white-and) done gone ballistic

all over the world, gone crazy, gone postal,

gone fishing, gone every goodbye but gone.

Ba-lues, Ba-lues (as in Basie's "Bleep, Blop, Blues")

say $e=mc^2$ (only inelegantly) don't equal much,

don't equal rights, don't equal action, don't

add up to nothing but slavery. Only this time

Ba-lues got plenty new niggers chained up:

Iraq, Iran, Afghanistan, Syria, Nigeria, Mexico—

plenty places Texaco can pull a Colombia, U-Haul

Yugoslavia (the former, that is), actively hate Haiti,

preach Jesus and, like a God who don't like ugly,

take this one out, put that one in. Ba-lues

taking names. Ba-lues' song say: "Bring 'em on!"

Ba-lues ain't letting nothing pass. Ba-lues kick ass

and laugh about it. Ba-lues don't care what it cost.

Ba-lues don't care nothing about loss. Truth, youth,

the Constitution, global resolutions, Simón Bolívar—

Ba-lues don't care nothing about freedom, declarations

of independence. Ba-lues in the democracy business.

Ba-lues run past you the terms of agreement for its

I Accept, I Do Not Accept democracy installations.

For males a Ba-lues tax cut means cutting your nuts;

clitoridectomy for females. No tickee, no laundry.

Ba-lues know if it ain't no money in the treasury, they

in the black, even if it's the white poor who get bled

out the red-white-and-blue. We spoilers. We victors.

Ba-lues gone ballistic. Ba-lues can't remember nothing

about Vietnam, the corporate scam, the millions

of bombs and people it's dropped; the CIA agents, the FBI,

the Agent Orange, the how now brown cow Dow

of chemistry, physics, the darkening pain of an insane

refrain. Ba-lues deals fear, Ba-lues deals jail, Ba-lues

allows only the news it chooses. Ba-lues know Uncle

Tom been done died. Ba-lues smooth your eyeball

with Dr. and Ms. Thomas. Ba-lues think tanks bankroll

books like *The Bell Curve*. All you boodie-call novelists,

get in line. Ba-lues' message to the world: "We still

know better than to give a nigger an inch. The lynch

mob, all electronic now, has jazz by night and anthrax

by day. Ba-lues got statistics. Ba-lues gone fascistic.

Ba-lues (as in red-white-and) done gone ballistic.

with an assist from O. O. Gabugah

33

Sundays in Democracies

for Peter Zimmels

Republicans: You're poor because
you're ignorant of all the laws
our Congress passed to cut the costs
of schooling children who get tossed,
nay, dumped upon society.
While we do view with piety
the right to life, we draw the line.
Clean up your act. To woo or wine
the loser class does not make sense.
Let's get this straight. We never winced
at taking public time to quarrel
with victims, thugs, the huge immoral
segment of the population
in our great, God-blessed, rich, free nation.

The Democrats: There was a time
the GOP and all its crime
got barely covered by the news,
which only aired *our* sins and blues.

What have they done for you, my friends?
Is making do or making ends
meet any measure of success?
We back the same Big Business mess
they do, but when we tighten your belt
we dig up Franklin Roosevelt.
We've given you prosperity
without their stark severity.
The only thing we have to fear?—
Republicans. Now, is that clear?

A Citizen: More parties, please,
more Sundays in democracies!
Each party dances, each side sings;
one great Big Bird with two right wings.
They'll boogie with you in the streets,
then drag you down to dark defeats.
Democracy? Look at our heroes:
CEO's billions, labor's zeroes—
pure DNA, unspliced and spliced.
If you think oil is over-priced,
consider what we're going to pay
for giving frequencies away—
the broadcast band. I say let's vote.
Let's kick some butt, let's rock some boat.

35

Lester Leaps In

Nobody but Lester let Lester leap
into a spotlight that got too hot
for him to handle, much less keep
under control like thirst in a drought.

He had his sensitive side, he had
his hat, that glamorous porkpie whose
sweatband soaked up all that bad
leftover energy.

       How did he choose
those winning titles he'd lay on favorites
—Sweets Edison, Sir Charles, Lady Day?
Oooo and his sound! Once you savor its
flaming smooth aftertaste, what do you say?

Here lived a man so hard and softspoken
he had to be cool enough to hold his horn
at angles as sharp as he was heartbroken
in order to blow what it's like being born.

Animal

That such an easing sound should make its moves
so smoothly on the tongue and in the flesh—
all padded paws, all cockatoos or hooves
—says something big about the ways we mesh.
Where once we granted soul its anima,
instinctively aware that raw volition
goes just so far (the same as stamina),
we worship bio-tech now; new religion.
The animal in ocean, jungle, stone—
we don't see with our eyes, but with our minds.
Intelligence, we think, is ours alone.
We smell, we groan, we pull our monkeyshines.
We speak and paint and dance and write and sing.
We snoop out landscapes where all bets are off,
where clothes stay packed and we, the King
and Queen of Soul, can do our stuff.
Maybe we love cartoons because they're us
except with anima put back in place.
These crazy ways we learn again to trust
the seal, the crocodile who wears our face.

A Low-Flying Blues for Somebody

TRACK 8

"Whoring my hands to move this military oil."
Gary Snyder, "T-2 Tanker Blues" *(Rip-Rap)*

In these hard and hardening times, poetry looks
and sees and then becomes an honest way to go.

To speak to one another rather than get talked to,
to listen to one another rather than one announcer,
to look out and see one another rather than be watched
and spied upon, and to touch and hold one another
rather than be handcuffed, imprisoned and shot—
what horrific differences. The unpublished picture
of a young, now legless G.I. mother, scrambling
on the floor with her three-year-old daughter (the Rock
of Gibraltar, the rock of Iraq) might make a defense
secretary or a secretary of state or a vice president
or an attorney general crack up secretly in laughter.

To rule the world you need you some oil. Crude but blunt
and right to the point. Cut to the Chase Manhattan of it,
barrelhouse the Bundesbank. Picture bales and bales
of hundred-dollar bills bundled up in Latin America's and others'
jungles, mildewed, rat-gnawed, pondering its own laundering.

In these hard and hardening times, poetry steps out and brings
back the deadest of giveaways, the cleanest of getaways.

Blues in December

Wasting money & running to the store,
seem like ain't nothin worth it no more—
Brew & turkey & sweet potato pie
How many years before I die?

Sit to rest & go on the nod,
shameful now in the eyes of God—
Weary & forgotten I'm scared I'll flip
If I don't take off on some trip

39

January

The VW needs serious transmission work,
the Datsun blows a radiator hose,
Blue Cross wants $425 right away,
the last checks of December come back
bouncing off the wall at $8.50 a crack,
the turntable quits spinning,
mildew overtakes the bathroom walls,
there's $50 worth of developed pictures
at Fotomat you can't afford to pick up,
the old typewriter's gonna cost $30
to fix up so you can rent it out.
You bite into an apple & hurt your molar
on the stem the same molar with root canal
work done last January & it's time
to go in for a checkup. They're gonna kick
you outta the screenwriters guild if
you don't pay up the 2 years' back dues.
The City of Los Angeles owes all
the money you spent in travel costs
to do a gig way back in November,
the radio you bought your son for graduation

fell apart & it's cheaper to buy a new one
than have his fixed, the Xmas briefcase
your wife gave you its handle's slipped off
already, prospects keep growing colder
as the water you're in grows hotter.
You know it's January when you have to stop
& pay close attention to what you're doing
wrong that seemed O so right last July.

Blue Monday

TRACK 9

The blues blow in their purity
more than minds; blues blow
through every sky and haunted heart
afloat. They say: I miss you, baby,
so I really went out and got drunk.

Blues say: Fool that I am, I jam
you in my toaster burning-brown

41

like bread on fire, blackening
in the Afro red Cadillac flame of love.

Blues say: Baby, you supposed to be.
Blues say: You supposed to be so big,
so bad, so slick. Quick! Tell me,
what is the distance from your heart
  to your dick?

Who I Am in Twilight

Like John Lee Hooker, like Lightnin Hopkins,
like the blues himself, the trickster sonnet,
hoedown, the tango, the cante jondo,
like blessed spirituals and ragas custom-made,
like sagas, like stories, like slick, slow,
sly soliloquies sliding into dramas,
like *Crime* & *Punishment*, like death & birth,
Canal Street, New Orleans, like the easy,
erasable, troubled voices a whirling

42

ceiling fan makes in deep summer nights in
hot, unheavenly hotels—Oklahoma, Arkansas,
Tennessee—like the Mississippi River
so deep and wide you couldn't get a letter
to the other side, like Grand Canyon,
like Yosemite National Park, like beans &
cornbread, like rest & recreation, like love
and like, I know we last. I know our bleeding stops.

Lost Passport Blues

TRACK 10

Travel never was what it used to be,
nor is to be or not to be a question
Buddhists can tackle, much less crack.
At dawn you wake up knowing
you will not make the flight.
Your geese are cooked; you've lost it:
your passport, the document that cements
your departures and arrivals, your exits

43

and entrances, your passing through doors
the way voyeurs see through stone and gut.
Vienna, with her stately elegance will not
see you today nor will she see you Monday,
an American holiday: Presidents Day.
To sunlight risen up and over trees
in California dances, breezeways,
you dedicate this morning. Poetry winks.
Who knows where your sacred passport
has traveled on its own? To what as yet
unknown locale? Before Columbus
cut his deal with the Crown of Castile,
who was lost? Who discovered what
or whom? Bottom-lines still dangle
on the buy-and-sell of it. "Passport?"
rude explorers declare. "We don't need
no stinking passports." Travel never was
what it used to be, nor is the here and now.

17–18 February 2007

44

Distances

To get to Tokyo from Istanbul,
it's fun to travel when the weather's cool.
To reach Madrid by way of Edinburgh,
it might be best to leave from Glockamorra.

The Shangri-La you dream about comes close
to meeting mute desire—an Ivory Coast,
the Gold Coast of the past, fountains of youth.
All colonies project a light from booths
in darkened rooms of mind; a picture forms
and moves and moves again and spills and warms
spaces between the heartbeat and held breath.

The distance anywhere—from birth to death,
from sit to stand, from heat to holy snow—
invents itself, unravels as you go.

Dear Old Stockholm

Of course it is snowing

but two city girls,

one blonde the other black-

haired, are preparing for bed

in a warm apartment they share.

One is washing her hair in the bathroom sink

while the other does hatha yoga exercises.

They have been dancing with some young men

who spoke nothing but north american english,

one of them from Pittsburgh

(from Crawford's Grill up on the Hill)

& the other

a fingerpopper from Leamington, Ontario.

Suddenly, recalling the evening,

the rushing from taxis up inside music clubs,

all of them pleased that it should be so,

the bathroom blonde

who,

like a great many Scandinavians,

played some instrument in secondary school

whistles John Coltrane's whole solo

from the Miles Davis *Dear Old Stockholm*

which had been an old Swedish folk song.

In fluorescent abandon

& in time

she massages her foamy scalp

with delight.

The young black-haired woman,

hearing all this

—tensed in a shoulderstand,

head full of new blood,

filling with new breath—

is overcome with unexpected happiness.

Each girl smiles in private

at the joyfulness of the evening

& at the music & the men, wishing

it would never end

47

The Old O.O. Blues

Like right now it's the summertime
    and I'm so all alone
I gots to blow some fonky rhyme
    on my mental saxophone

Brother Trane done did his thang
    and so have Wes Montgomery,
both heavyweights in the music rang,
    now I'mo play my summary

It's lotsa yall that thank yall white
    (ought I say European?)
who thank Mozart and Bach's all right,
    denyin your Black bein

Well, honkyphiles, yall's day done come,
    I mean we gon clean house
and rid the earth of Oreo scum
    that put down Fats for Faust

This here's one for-real revolution
  where ain't nobody playin
We intends to stop this cultural pollution
  Can yall git to what I'm sayin?

Sittin up there in your Dior gown
  and Pierre Cardin suit
downtown where all them devil clowns
  hang out and they ain't poot!

We take the white man's bread and grants
  but do our own thang with it
while yall bees itchin to git in they pants
  and taint the true Black spirit

I'm blowin for Bird and Dinah and Billie,
  for Satch, Sam Cooke, and Otis,
for Clifford, Eric, and Trane outta Philly
  who split on moment's notice

49

Chump, you ain't gon never change,
  your narrow ass is sankin
Like Watergate, your shit is strange
  You drownin while we thankin

My simple song might not have class
  but you can't listen with impunity
We out to smash your bourgeois ass
  and by *we* I mean The Community!

Uncle Sam Ain't No Woman, Take 2

"Uncle Sam ain't no woman,
but he sure can take your man."
Traditional blues verse
as sung by Blind Snooks Eaglin

Uncle Sam still ain't no woman,
but he can still take your man.
And he'll take your woman besides.

Take her by surprise, and take the fifth
in court. Boo, gotcha again!
So you got a problem with that?

Uncle Sam take you to the cleaners,
too, you mess with him, you signify.
No lie. Die now or die later, the sooner

the better. Uncle Sam ain't no woman.
He ain't no uncle no more, either.
He ain't for no fresh air, he ain't for no breather.

51

The Indiana Gig

In glassy, incandescent glory
the ascent hastens me home
all over again; a gig is a gig.
But something real & big looms here.
You can see it woven into the warp
of light & sound around the edges
of this morning. The way that dog
is woofing across the grassy lot
of dawn & up behind the sycamores.
Home was never a place to begin with,
but sly effulgence that keeps
leaking & looking out from nowhere.

Sometimes you sound it as "Back Home
in Indiana," other times it's Miles'
"Donna Lee," but always, always
there's a Hoosier drowsiness
spread in lazy splendor out across
the soul's industrial, farmed-out heartland.
To catch it completely, it's sometimes
necessary to drop down an octave,
hear it as being downsouth, only breezier,

& the flight's almost complete.
You're ready to turn as red as any leaf
in the Indiana summer of playful lemonade,
axle grease, corn & tractored slow ball.

Dead Moth Blues

Moths fall and crawl, then die outside your door.
Sometimes they look like tiny folded fans,
their spots and coloration all the more
attractive than they seem when one moth lands
on one bright bulb or some somber flame.

You came home from some outing in your youth
and there on your doormat—unclaimed, unnamed—
a dead moth lay. Your body knew the truth:
the world had changed. You copped to this somehow.

Now years have changed. You understand the deal.
Your feet take heed, they don't dare fail you now;
they wipe themselves. They know how death is real.

Threshholds and backdoors, icy steel beams, soft cloths
—they all go missing. Caterpillars. Moths.

Giving the Drummer Some

TRACK 12

L.H.O.O.Q.
(pronounced: *Elle a chaude au cul*)
Early 20th century "ready-made"
by Marcel Duchamp

She's all fucked up and French, he knows.
He knows the cultural pressure she's under,
knows what she's started, knows what won't end.
The big sky color of her eyes, the European
complication she's hooked into, all that shit,

he knows it well. At first he didn't know much French,
but he got it together pretty quick. He got the rhythm
of it, its round and nasal loveliness, the underflow,
the way sometimes she sounded like a horn; other
times like reeds. There'd been a point he'd read about
when the Mediterranean had been like a Muslim lake;
the Moors had come that close to taking France.
Now here they were again. Back. And standing
unbathed, backless, blue, bikini'd, blunt—her butt:
two round vowels not yet moist with towels because
she liked the sound of funky in her proud tongue—
fon-quiii as you wanna be, gallant Gallic mama!
How long could he hang in Paris between gigs
How thick did he wish to get with Klook
and Griff and Kenny and Dexter and Mal
and, before them, Don Byas, Sidney Bechet?
Steve Lacy had hipped him when he'd first hit town:
"Dance, man. Do your dance and keep moving."
For a class drummer, he figured, I ain't doing bad.
It wasn't the French invented surrealism; it was Americans.
Jazz, too. It was time to drag Monique, he decided,
over to the stereophonique to debut his new CD.
As Romeo once said to Juliet, "Haven't we met?"
He had no doubt that he could straighten her out.

Moss

The Rolling Stones,
a hard English group,
busted for heroin
at their Southern France estate,
fifty grams of smack a week
said the man on the news
just to keep
their little family extended

Well, so what,
what'll happen to them?
So what if the air
back of these superstars
gets waved away
from time to time
like those costly backdrops
in the old film factories?

Charles Christopher Parker,
a genius among geniuses,
was granted diplomatic immunity
the moment that he died

Eleanora Fagan Gough
(the Billie Holiday who now
powers many a Silver Cloud)
was a sufferer among sufferers
with narks up in her deathbed

Even Bela Lugosi,
our beloved Transylvanian,
sustained his habit in real life
& metaphorically on screen

Ah the Rolling Stones,
a hard English group,
heroes of an American era

Green Death Blues

Was it the girl or was it the ale? Thousands and thousands of sundowns later, he still couldn't tell. What he recalls: When he gazed across the water from where he, his wife, their kindergartener son and another family were setting up camp for the weekend, his eye had been drawn to a young woman who stood at the fern-greened shore, reflective and alone, clutching a quart bottle of Rainier Ale.

Rainier Ale, whose street and party name was Green Death, had been one of his youthful companions and comforts. The heroin of beers, he called it. Clearly this shapely, pale woman—her red hair long, her bedspread dress dragging the riverbank—lived around there. He sized her up as a country hippie, a north coast hippie. Van Damme State Park was near Mendocino on the edge of the Little River. It was the mid-1970s. By then the Sixties that people now like to talk about so recklessly were breathing down necks down full bore, going great guns.

The way she up-ended her sunset-lit bottle told him she loved the stuff. From time to time she held the bottle out in front of her, presumably to note how much ale was left. Most sensible beer-drinkers did not like Green Death. "My tongue gets thick," a buddy once told him. "I start slurring my words. After I've knocked back two little cans of Rainier Ale, I start wobbling on my feet. Hell, I can practically put away a whole six-pack of Bud or Miller's before I feel anything like a buzz. But Green Death—it's ruthless."

When he saw her wipe her lips with the back of her hip-resting hand, then look across the river, but not at him, he guessed that she was having what

Henry James' philosopher brother, William James, might have called the varieties of religious experience. The observation backed his theory of how the term church-key—a commonly used beer can or beer bottle opener prior to the introduction of twist-offs and pop-tops—drifted into the language. For many perhaps, the closest they ever come to tasting some form of religion or entering a transcendental or mystical state is in the ingestion of beer, which he knew dated all the way back to ancient Egypt and to Sumerian culture, Southern Iraq, dating back five thousand years—that we know of.

Those who did the grunt-work on the Pyramids at Giza are said to have been paid in beer and in salt. We get the word salary from the Latin word for salt. Speakers of Spanish still say sal. He had once sat with his pal Charlie Washington at the Haight Street Bar-B-Q in the Fillmore District and watched Jesse "Lone Cat" Fuller, shake salt into his glass of beer. Jesse, a one-man band (twelve-string guitar, harmonica, kazoo and a homemade, foot-driven bass-like contraption that Jesse called the footdella) was one of his folk music heroes.

All of this shot through his mind while he watched the woman savor her brew of choice on the banks of the Little River. The little mind-movie he'd shot way back then still plays in the darkened theater of his imagination.

He had watched her so closely from that watery distance that some of their energy might have merged. Observer and observed interact and intersect. He almost never poured himself another Rainier Ale without thinking of what he now remembered as her lovable presence. How roundly memory smoothes down the years. A few years following the Mendocino camping trip, he came back home from home to a one-semester teaching gig in Texas to learn that his favorite columnist, the San Francisco Chronicle's Charles McCabe had died.

McCabe, who actually wrote columns about his passion for Green Death, was found dead in his apartment. Sadly it had been his daughter who'd found him. McCabe had evidently tripped and fallen, striking his head against some object sharp enough to cause a fatal concussion. He had clipped and filed away some of Mr. McCabe's columns. He uncovered some that sang the man's praises for Rainier Ale. McCabe loved the taste and bite of it; other beers left him flat.

McCabe likened Rainier to some of the heavy, dark European beers he savored. With its brooding brunette color and pleasing bitter vim, Green Death was sometimes as much fun to look at as it was to imbibe. McCabe had once described how he rose in the wee hours, then got himself over to Chronicle head-quarters at Fifth and Mission, where he worked on his 700-word column. Once it was finished, usually by 5 a.m., McCabe would then repair to the bar across the street, where other reporters and other Chron personnel gathered. There he would put away several ales, then head home to sleep. Maybe he didn't get up and go to the office after all. Maybe McCabe was slyly telling us that he composed his column at the close of a hard day's night. However other readers interpreted it, he knew that the Jesuit-trained McCabe was one odd and interesting newspaper-man.

Before it got moved to the features section, McCabe's energetic column appeared in the sports section, which, in those days, was printed on green pages. The Fearless Spectator, he called it, before changing it to Charles McCabe Himself. What fearful and fearless spectators we each become in the unexpected presence of events or spectacles that strike us as strange, or all too close to home.

The Old-Fashioned Cincinnati Blues

for Jesse "Lone Cat" Fuller

O boy the blues!
I sure do love blues
but the blues don't like me

This is Cincinnata Ohia 1949
& that's me & my brother Frank
in the NY Central Train Station
trying to get it together
on our way down
to Meridian Mississippi
where later I hid
in cornfields, smoked butts &
dreamed all about
the sunny grownup future,
dreamed about Now

Ah but that Now that
Right Now that is,

all I wanna dream about's
that NY Cincy Terminal
that summer with its intervals
of RC Cola Coolers,
tin tub baths taken
one at a time
back behind the evening stove—

Chickens—

Our grandmother
(Mrs Lillian Campbell)—

Cousin George & Uncle John
swapping ghost stories
Saturday nite—

O Americana!
United Statesiana!

A lonesome high,
a funnytime cry,
the blues
the blues
the blues

Ruby My Dear

Thelonious Monk, 1959

You are back again, re-entering the central train of trails: the quintessential U.S.A. of drowsy fields and sleepy fast-food chains, the U.S.A. of nipped buds and layaways negotiated in harsh, flatland cracker accents. Surrounded by them, hemmed in, you sometimes feel a little like one of those brainy slicksters over at the federal penitentiary in Milan, Michigan, for, like them, you're locked up and keyed down.

"Ruby My Dear" comes drifting down Lake Huron in the saline marshlands of an eternal summer. The Midwestern night is steamy hot with mosquitoes, then air knotted and thick with gnats like Monk's gracefully gnarled chordal clusters; notes and spiraling nodes, encoded, glistening like Milky Way–encrusted swirls and specks of darkness.

You know what you're hearing is human yearning and rushes of the Divine calling you home to all the Africanized galaxies in this shimmering island universe.

Five

in memory of pianist Bill Evans

(1929–1980)

1/

In quiet, well-grazed groves,
up trees no player need reach,
some young squirrels,
scampering on breadfruit alone,
feel and even know they are forsaken
the way it ought to be for feeders.

2/

Out in the low fields at night
no one knew which way to turn
for canteloupe—
but watermelon, hey, don't you know?
All those seeds, all that red,
all that sugar going, "Juice, Juice, Juice!"
Oooo, the wet ripe rhapsody of fruit.

3/

Did somebody's child just rediscover moonlight?
Where would any of us be without that stuff?
What player hasn't hit that lick
a hundred times at least? What light
hasn't shone through keyboards under glass,
the sea an octave away? Smother me
under your pillowing spell.
Roll me in the dirty boogie-woogie of your light.

4/

O go for it! You can't fake these ultra-rhythms,
or can you? The way, the road, the distance
to Bali is the same as to Cairo. Karo Syrup
yourself all over like June. Bust out, break
free. Can the beat be everything? Maybe not,
but this is where we either jump back or
kick down the gate. Fax that back to Heaven.

5/

Hello, rain, so it's you again,

this time deluging Duluth. So where

do we go from here? What kind of thunder

are you putting us under this time?

Maple leaf don't stand a chance. And, birch,

forget it. There is in your attitude

and lean a summer just begun yet all but gone.

In telling squalls you make your soft, moist points.

Squashed by stars and hills and green air,

paned and spaced or squeezed between clouds,

we're moving now; call off your waltz.

Count off your classy blues and count us in.

The station's sounding smaller as we go.

The clouds we've shaped. The smile, the wave

the lake makes feels hipper too. Some gig!

Sweet sleep, slide slowly, gently, cleanly

through this bubbling blood of ours.

See, See, Moon

See, see, moon, O see what you done done
(or is it done did?) I don't know
the right way to talk to you no more,
nor do I care that you don't answer me.
I've walked into rooms, their windows
overflowed with light & fresh air
& understood how big plugs of skylessness
can get translated into versions of illusion;
blinded beauty in all its fullness.

*   *   *

But when the blues overtakes you,
every little once in while,
bluegummed moon, all explanations fail
it seems, but no, the blues
by any other name would be
just as funky.
Why should it be so difficult
to pin the color of your sorrow?

67

Saudades: The Portuguese Blues

TRACK 13

Perched at the railing of a Portuguese
freighter, frightened inside, wavelengths
from home and known to no one here
except the not so secret police,
I'm struck by how that brownskinned girl
in a moon-knit dress and Sunday pumps
beams from the pier below. Already I know
next to nothing about her, and soon
I'll know even less. But nothing
could've possibly prepared me for her
long-distance smile that gently bridges
the mileage anywhere. How can I not be
gladdened by sharing the way she shines
in the late Lisbon night; a quivering
blue glow seeping into the deep
and rolling sea? Just see how she sways
and waves at the sight of her father
the seaman, the ship's wireless operator

positioned just now at my left, right
beside me. He's back in contact
with his proudest connection: this
motherless angel he's been bragging about
like a daddy all the way over from steamy
Brooklyn to the shores of the Azores, and
on to the mainland and islands of me.

Shaken to discover myself so removed
from all the family I've ever known,
I couldn't be happier than I am now,
watching him hurry down the gangplank home.
They charge into each other's arms and then,
peering up, squinting, shading his eyes,
he signals me his last farewell. Ah, well,
this is where I become a stranger again;
an unraveled, woolly-minded, off-season
traveler all decked out with no place else
to go and no one to answer at these ports
of call. Soon we'll be free to be memories
of each other. But for one skylit minute—
radiant and radio clear—another part
of my head snaps on, it begins to crackle
with a pop song from long ago about kisses
and fundamental things. And time and I

go drifting by; we flow with the last
of the cool, salty light out across
the dark dock water that cradles this
crusty old boat. In fact, as I shoulder
my pack of belongings, a longing
overcomes me and for chorus after chorus
I can still feel that flow; feel it
pulling us apart; feel it nudging
the swollen summer toward fall. Sighing,
descending now; I can even feel how time
will feel as it lightens my momentary
burden of being all too young, all too
wise, and far too deliriously alone.

My Spanish Heart

TRACKS 14–15

after Chick Corea

In audible dreams I'm forever going back
to Spain. Now, tell me what that's all about?
Perhaps in some past life or lives I lived
there and cared about the African presence
in Iberia or New Iberia, eh? Get serious!
It's probably because all my life I've been
an all-nite sucker for spicy rhythm ticking
and booming away like an afro-latinized gypsy
taxi meter waiting to be fed that long mileage.
Whatever the reason or rhyme, I can think of
no better fate than to end up masking my nights
in the gardens of Spain—and how Spanish is
Spain?—with a warm, bubbling, undreamed lady
whose dark-throated murmuring is song. Picture
it: Just a couple of music lovers, all but
wasting in moonlight, with poetry damp and cooling
right up under our noses, soft lips, a mustache
—Ay, the possibilities of Spanish, the loving
tongue! Listen . . . "Adiós, adiós, mi corazón."

71

Dexter

for Dick & Sarah Maxwell

In slow-blowing zones
the dream floats on
tough
unbitten
nail-hard swiftness

Catnapped
the beat expands
to match a scratchy brush stroke

Drummers
beware

Clearing the Way for Ecstasy

TRACK 16

Big skies have always hung around in bursts
of peril and merriment. Such lush urgency.

Warm fast beside me on the floor, unemerged,
you press your body-you into my body-me:
a mass of space and particles, a cloud of chords
and song still unarranged, massive; a crowd
of two so undemonstrative we don't get attacked
by cops with real or rubber bullets, with M-16's
or mace—not yet. Your fingers laced in mine
design the interlocking force that glues galaxies.

Big skies above our rooftop spread and clear
the way for ecstasy, a thunderhead to break
our sense of wonder away from one another,
to turn back into lake and sea the stream
your body-you, my body-me must have

73

always been. Of all the civilians voluptuously
curled up on this rug so randomly—why us?

How can anyone, you ask, how can anyone kill
in such surroundings of desert, mountain, jungle,
savannah, plains, delta, beach, shore, star
and all the light that scraps us into birth? I listen.

To cello, drums and soulful shouts we brush
against the grain. You gun your thrusts and
time yourself to me. I give up every time.

Big skies will always hang around in bursts
of peril and merriment. Such hushed urgency.

74

Body and Soul: 16 Minutes, 59 Seconds

in memory of Dexter Gordon

Back when time was thick and money scarce,
you got your shit together fast and sweet.
Now that you can stretch, love rubbernecks

her way through every nook and cranberry
you can finger, every cocktail your nighttime
can contain. At intervals. Ahhh, mmmmm.

We love to do the curlicue, the poco loco
baroque on stuff like this: big passion-perfected
practices our world-wearying staleness styles.

Years wear thin. In thorns of joy we turn up
all crowned down: the Body and Soul of time.
Why were they, why were we, why were you born?

We lay off into what we've got down pat,

or all we know of love. But that's no fun.

"Hey, Body," it says. "Hey, Soul. Three minutes

to go. Hey, baby!" We swallow it, wallowing

whole, wallowing wide. In his stupendously delayed

decay, Dexter broke and mended our hearts.

Step Out on the Tightrope and Don't Look Down

*"Each time I play, I step out on
the tightrope and don't look down."*
Marian McPartland

There were problems, problems, problems, and she had them
almost down. Mastering the languages of daylight helped
her make it through the night, 98.6 percent. Tunisia didn't count.

She didn't think she could write melody, only arrangements—
or so she thought. It was largely personal, hugely undigital.
How do you carve an elephant out of a block of granite?
You get rid of all the parts that aren't an elephant.
And so in the days when music wasn't everywhere, she sat in
a little joint where she could drink coffee and nosh.
She scribbled one dozen poems in one night, each one a classic;
each designated, destined to be anthology fodder. Set to music,
two turned into hits for singers who, like her, worked best
without a net. Big money, big problems; big headaches, big dookey
whizzed in and she grabbed at them the way a high wire
artist might grab at a hot wire on no notice, no nod, no notion
of what lies ahead. Seen clearly, daylight moved back in
and problems blacked out into their blameless blue origins.
"Once again," she told the press, "I bow to the Muse."
Was her Muse the blues? How many falses? How many trues?

Straight No Chaser

TRACK 17

Well, Monk said it straight:
It's out of town when you wait...
He knew the answer;
The town's a dancer.
You know you can't pack up the moment
And take it with you on the road,
So now is the time.
Sally Swisher
(from the blues, *"Get It Straight";*
instrumentally known as
"Straight No Chaser")

What wound up seeming strange to you was me.

But why? You bad-mouthed me all over town,

then turned around and asked me if I'd be

your lover one more time. So we got down.

It felt real good. Baby, didn't it? Being real?

Our river overflowed, our tree limbs shook.

The woods, a stormy sky—hey, no big deal!

I wrapped myself around you, then you took

your own sweet time and mine coming unglued.

Pinned down that way, I couldn't tell you off.

You broke our bond, but stuck there in the mood.

To woo or not to woo? My voice went soft.

We slept all slow, got back to work by ten.

I bet you're wondering if I'll call again

Conjugal Visits

TRACK 18

By noon we'll be deep into it—
  up reading out loud in bed.
Or in between our making love
  I'll paint my toenails red.

Reece say he got to change his name
  from Maurice to Malik.
He think I need to change mine too.
  Conversion, so to speak.

"I ain't no Muslim yet," I say.
  "Besides, I like my name.
Kamisha still sounds good to me.
  I'll let you play that game."

"I'd rather play with you," he say,
  "than trip back to the Sixties."
"The Sixties, eh?" I'm on his case.
  "Then I won't do my striptease."

This brother look at me and laugh;
  he know I love him bad
and, worse, he know exactly how
  much loving I ain't had.

He grab me by my puffed up waist
  and pull me to him close.
He say, "I want you in my face.
  Or on my face, Miss Toes."

What can I say? I'd lie for Reece,
  but I'm not quitting school.
Four mouths to feed, not counting mine.
  Let Urban Studies rule!

I met him in the want ads,
  we fell in love by mail.
I say, when people bring this up,
  "Wasn't no one up for sale."

All these Black men crammed up in jail,
  all this I.Q. on ice,
while governments, bank presidents,
  the Mafia don't think twice.

They fly in dope and make real sure
  they hands stay nice and clean.
The chump-change Reece made on the street
  —what's that supposed to mean?

"For what it costs the State to keep
  you locked down, clothed and fed,
you could be learning Harvard stuff,
  and brilliant skills," I said.

Reece say, "Just kiss me one more time,
  then let's get down, make love.
Then let's devour that special meal
  I wish they'd serve more of."

They say the third time out's a charm;
  I kinda think they're right.
My first, he was the Ace of Swords,
  which didn't make him no knight.

He gave me Zeus and Brittany;
  my second left me twins.
This third one ain't about no luck;
  we're honeymooners. Friends.

I go see Maurice once a month
  while Moms looks after things.
We be so glad to touch again,
  I dance, he grins, he sings.

When I get back home to my kids,
  schoolwork, The Copy Shop,
ain't no way Reece can mess with me.
  They got his ass locked up.

Prelude to a Kiss

in memory of Ella Fitzgerald

There was a time when singing or playing a ballad was almost the same as the whisper your lips make the instant before they pooch out and stretch, then reach to touch hers.

Her lips will feel the warm wind your whisper makes in the life-preserving urgency of moving mouth-to-mouth. Whole career moves, investments have been based on this, a kiss.

There at the after-whisper—when breath saith unto breath: "Death, go back out and wait in the car, baby, we got some unfinished business we need to take care of up in here"—there Ben Webster or Lester might pester you into listening to thrilling snapshots of their up-close worlds, where rivers and stars and cyclones and witch-hunts and hatred found and hounded them endlessly. But Ella's voice would graze the words and say: Psssst-psssst and Shhh-shhh.

Whenever Body Snatchers invaded, remember? Remember the Memorex commercial? Shattered, the glass itself was thinking: "Better this way than whoops! Better this than drunk-ass fans arguing. Who was best—Billie, Sarah, Dinah, Carmen or Ella?"

There she stood, or there she sat at piano, not playing, sometimes in pain—a twisted ankle, a mangled heart—wiggling around on that bench, whispering her bloodbeat to crowds in Spain, Brazil, Japan, the Netherlands, Australia, Oslo, L.A., Akron, Accra, Krakow, and O how they knew when her voice—a whip, a feather—was busy inventing universes they always thought had been in place all along.

Wrong. Ella Fitzgerald launched songs far more reliably than NASA launched spacecraft. She sent them spinning into orbits that ennobled, that ran rainbows around your shoulders.

We couldn't carry her around in that basket forever. Ella owned the world the way she earned our owning her. Every time her voice floats back, that kiss moves in, and then begins.

The Leadbelly Song

Yes I'm glad

blood signature or no

& that walking

you talk about

I done all that

walked all the way

from Detroit

to California

& didn't stop once

to pluck the thorns

out of my brain,

met some pretty gals,

kissed to the song

went to war

a photograph of me

on one side

& on the other

in the distance

snorting like a stuck bull

myself in flames

stomping forward

to tangle ass

a bomb went off

cherry smelling,

got guitars thrown at me

& I was spared

the chain gang

ah, but you could sing

cities & ashes

& brown/black/meat

wobbling thru your songs

bullets flying

western cowboys

the space between

train tracks

widening before us

green grass

corn

heaven

pictures & energy

pouring from you

like rainwater

trickling down a branch

I caught the fever

called off the war

put everything away

stopped walking

stopped talking

moved in with Jean Harlow

bought that horse

Stewball

on a Monday

& kissed Irene

goodnight

flopped over

grew my hair out

picked up on your jive

fingers tingling

wrapped around

a new hammer

The Midnight Special Revisited

Mean old murderous Leadbelly,
Sugarland bound as sure as you're born,
no longer buzzard lopes down Fannin Street
with hat, tin can & razor in hand
in the company of another Jeffersonian,
the one known to blues hounds, white cops
& redlight sisters as Blind Lemon.
It was them yella women who finally ran
the two of them outta Houston, they say,
& it was over that long overdue long green.

Fannin Street acts like a boulevard now;
skimpy skyscrapers, condos & hospitals
& banks shadow its haunted, motorized length.
Sugarland's no longer a catch-all prison;
it's a high security suburb now, housing
a brand new kind of convict: the managerial
elite with some pro athletes thrown in.
Neither Negro nor Jew nor White Folks sing
or gather in its streets to celebrate
or do much of anything except meet the Metro.
Besides, there is no town downtown

beyond rush hour. Only Montrose boasts
of Street People & the crime rate there
is closely watched. Seriously, you'd
have to hot tail it all the way back to when
gasoline was 15 cents a gallon to find
so much as a watermelon man or a hot tamale man
or a strolling spasm band on Fannin Street.
Even the hustling gals work out of XXX'd up
stucco nudie joints now, like the one next
door to the nursery school you bike past.
But the KKK is still alive & thriving.
Christian born-againers still burn
& the fervor of their flaming return
to fundamentals crisscrosses the topless
pistol shot nights & crackles the way
lightning always splinters God's Country
—with Texan Amurican splendor.
Religious, political or not, the cops'll
still gitcha if you don't watch out!
They catch you acting too colored or
not colored enough—it's blam!
You better not stagger & you better not fight
'cause the only Miss Rosie you're liable
to see won't be coming to bail nobody
outta nowhere. As a matter of fact,

chances are the umbrella on her shoulder
& that piece of paper in her hand
will only mean she's doubling as Weather
& Anchor person tonight on the Six O'Clock News.

Up Vernon's Alley

for the great bassist Vernon Alley

His smile can light up wood as good as pluck.

All spark, no match, his finger's on some fuse

hooked up to soul; an ammunition truck.

Whole worlds go up when Vernon plays the blues.

Sweet Sixteen Lines

You bet it would've made a tender movie!
If only someone had been flighty enough
to capture the shape of what turned out to be
our last days alone, the end of a rough
journey that dulled every sense but touch.
Heroically juvenile, lighter than light,
we talked what we felt, but never thought much.
We were Romeo and Juliet night after night.
It was like we'd sailed from heaven in a jet,
copilots, cool but glorious, and landed
our sullen craft too artfully—poets yet;
runaways on life's slick runway of expanded
unconsciousness. Maybe. Who knows for sure?
But Ruby and the Romantics came out that year
with a sweet-nothing single: hot, airy and pure
enough to hold us aloft by heart and by ear.

The Pianist Prepares Her Playlist

To a world stuck on cutting corners to reach shallow conclusions
she played juicy bebop piano, she hedged her tunes to satisfy lovers
and defectors alike. She wondered. To defect from love, to opt out—

could it be done? When did you leave? Which way did you run?
The consummate music-mathematician, she knew and understood.
The answers, all multiple, stalked the cracks between the keys

she touched and modulated. Like honeycombs of ants, her playlists
sent out scouts & put out feelers. Their ins & outs skated & swam
on feeling: how the room felt, how the night felt, how the whole country

felt about wasting life; how national security was all about killing,
rarely about life-saving, never about giving, never about hope,
never about need, always about greed. The news she caught afternoons

when she got up sketched chords and rhythms to her pulse; stretched
imagination ("It's silly, you go around willy-nilly"). Before the gig
she rehearsed her playlist & left it open to massive last-minute changes.

We might even be in the final hours, she sometimes imagined.
Thank God for music for something spirit wraps itself around;
a sound investment pre-approved & with nothing but payoff.

She got it that you had to play for people what they need to hear,
which sometimes wasn't what you felt like playing. Juicy, joy-giving
bebop: a hop, skip & more than a jump from what you meant

to what you actually say. The room was hers. By giving, she got.
By pushing love, she pulled all boundaries apart. Her politics:
the beat, her heart. Her dragnet: love all wet, magnetic & ready.

Los Angeles, Los Angeles: One Long-Shot, One Cutaway

TRACK 19

1/

Inside your belly, a new beast ripens.

While all your twilit litters guard the door,

the ghost of Ho Chi Minh pours out a toast:

Here's to old Saigon, Taiwan, Hong Kong, Beijing;

Iran before the Shah; to Port-au-Prince,

and Port of Spain, Tijuana, Kingston Town;

to Tokyo, Bombay, Tel-Aviv, Nairobi and Accra.

Not Ghana but the oldest Gold Coast drums

her thoughts out loud in not so cooling colors,

The darkest nights of Seoul turn into tunnels,

where rays of hope, spaghetti thin, break skin

and ream the veins of dreams so long deferred

that laser-lined Thought Police 100 years from now

still can't decrypt the meaning of their blood;

    their blues.

2/

A Stoli on the rocks, some rock cocaine,

a spoon of smack can crack the sound of barriers

and barrios alike. But light is hard.

Prez in Paris, 1959

By 1959 he'd moved to Paris.
Prez wouldn't eat. Sweet alcohol harassed
his system. Cooled, the jazz "To Be or Not
to Be"—withdrawn, a whisper—seemed a jot.

Once there'd been ways to get back at the world;
Ex-G.I. Prez had tried and tired. He hurled
himself now—hearsay, smoky horn—down-stage.
"Well, Lady Gay Paree, it's been a dog's age,"

he might've said. Or "Ivy Divey! Wrong!
The way that channel swims—too cold. This song
—the lyric's weak. We'll drown. No eyes, my man.
No, let's don't take it from no top. The band

can skip it." Prez. Monsieur le Président,
who played us what can work, and what just won't.

Detroit 1958

Only parts of the pain of living
may be captured in a poem or
tale or song or in the image seen.

Even in life we only halfway feel
the tears of a brother or sister,
mass disenchantment in cities,
our discovery of love's meagerness,
the slow rise and fall of the sun.

Sadness is the theme of existence;
joy its variations. Pain is only a portion
of sadness, and efforts to escape it
can lead to self-destruction,
one aspect of pain lived imaginatively.

It is in life that we celebrate pain;
It is in art that we imitate it,

Beauty is saddening, or, as the man sings,
"The bitter note makes the song so sweet."

A Poem for Lena Horne

And when it came down to Negro nights,

those Colored Only slices in time,

you took the cake, Lena, & ran

& danced with it, O! You were so gorgeous

they didn't know what to do with you,

those not so gentle men at MGM & elsewhere.

Where else but in the USA's of the world

would it go on record that you & Ava

Gardner used to knock back a few

in the palmy hours, laughing over how

the studio would darken her up from head

to toe to lipsynch & mouth the sound

of your voice for Showboat. Hurray

for Hollywood! The jewel blue you

will never be seen, only heard in the role

of Miss Julie, the octoroon swooning

under the June-jazzed Dixiemental moon.

You can laugh about it now & soften the sting.

You can smile & even do a step or two & sing

& I suppose you haven't done bad, given

your class & origins & given the almighty odds

& the gods of showbiz heaven who own, control

& chart the color of beauty & its stars.

Tell me again about the time your numbers

banker daddy told Samuel Goldwyn he'd be happy

to pay for your maids & upkeep since

you didn't have sense enough to understand

the movies didn't have much use for people

of your hue. They stashed you in some doozies

too—*Panama Hattie*, *As Thousands Cheer*,

I Dood It, *Swing Fever*, *Two Girls* & *a Sailor*,

but the trick was to tailor you for the South.

How did they do it? Well, wasn't much to it.

They'd log you in, then chop you out (like

lumber) for the slumbering southern houses.

I knew your son Ted, a fledgling writer, dead

to you these many years. You outlived him,

your husband and your dad who all moved out

in the very same year. I can almost hear—

sometimes when you sing—the strong & lasting

side of you that once told Billie Holiday

she had to learn to be tough, that these hucksters

didn't mean no man no good, let alone womanhood.

You're still lovely, Lena. Moms Mabley was wrong.

The rubberbands she said were holding your face up

are never going to snap. You are the song.

Ava, She Was One of Your Women

An MGM property, as she later stated,
"None of us was ever very well educated."
For one hundred bucks a week each,
the studio knew it could afford to reach
deep into future space for its heroines, its stars.
You can talk about your Hedy Lamarrs,
your Lanas, your Grables, your Ritas, your Janes,
but none of those well-screened women sustains
your interest the crazy way Ava Gardner
did and still does. Ava was your partner—
no satiny matinee idolatress, either.
She calmed the hot and heavy breather
in you. Sexual, intellectual, aristocratic,
she drew you woofully into the ecstatic,
where feeling and thought, like energy and mass,
squared up, imploded; imagination, class,
were everything; knowledge a way-station.
She filled in blanks for you. Your education
owed as much to *The Snows of Kilimanjaro*

101

as it did to the steamy straight-and-narrow that
contessas didn't walk barefoot. With Artie Shaw
Ava learned how great books worked. She saw
how what you hear and see and say and feel
grows deep when you and you alone get real.
Ideas? You had to bounce them, see which way
they fell into your world. Ava moved to Spain
and then to London, where the supple pain
of being a star, a ghost impression, slowed.
What was it about Ava that pulled and glowed,
that yanks and warms the eye and heart today
in a century she never reached to shrug away?

Rush

She missed the lavish hush and swish,
the cool, safe sound of leaves on trees
in streets where they'd been rich.
She missed the festive breeze
fame swept her up in. No costly drink,
no posh cuisine could even hold a candle
to the thrill of trembling on the brink
of sudden stardom, a bitch to handle.
Granted. But she'd loved it. Bigtime.

She missed their flashy swimming pool;
its drop-dead size and shape, the climb
back out, the diving in, the warming jewel-
like look of light across the tiles.
She missed it all: the deals, the studio calls,
make-up, shoots, interviews, the hype. Files
of clippings, fan mail, scripts, her dizzy walls
lonely with snapshots, big posters in French,
Italian, Polish, Japanese—cold keepsakes,
maybe, but they laid it out. Inch by inch
they proved she'd won the only sweepstakes

that count. She'd done it twice in this icy

town where, win or lose, just don't you miss the boat.

The killing cost of what she missed (pricey

barely said it), even that didn't float

far in her shoreless sea of gut-deep blues.

She missed the in-your-face power-rush

reality of celebrity. And she would choose

those streets again; the swish, the loving hush.

Groupie

Evening isn't so much a playland as it is
a rumpus room, a place where harmony
isn't always complementary & where
spaces between palmtrees of the heart
aren't always so spread out.

By 3 a.m.
there's love in her hose for the sailor
of saxophones or guitars & she'll try & take
the whole night into her skilled mouth
as tho that were the lover she really wanted
to rub against when all the time true love
inhabits her own fingernails & unshaven body.

You love her for the mental whore she is,
the clothed sun in Libra, the horny sister
who with her loose hair flying can get
no better attention for the time being.

Hot House

Embryonic or symphonic
the sun on glass effect
of this rhythm is torrid

Florid in their nearness
fragrant light reigns
& slow time breathes

Even the orchid has
catches: an orchestra
hides in her color, her O

Sweet conjugal love is
not beyond this sound
where New York meets Puri

In the softest blur
of time & its rivers
the heat of dreams arrives

The James Cotton Band at Keystone

TRACK 21

And the blues, I tell you, they blew up
on target; blew the roof right off
& went whistling skyward, starward,
stilling every zooming one of us
mojo'd in the room that night, that
instant, that whenever-it-was. Torn
inside at first, we all got turned out,
twisting in a blooming space where
afternoon & evening fused like Adam
with Eve. The joyful urge to cry
mushroomed into a blinding cloudburst
of spirit wired for sound, then atomized
into one long, thunderous, cooling downpour.

What ceased to be was now & now & now.
Time somehow was what the blues froze

107

tight like an underground pipe before

busting it loose in glad explosions; a

blast that shattered us—ice, flow & all.

The drift of what we'd been began to

shift, dragging us neither upstream nor

down but lifting us, safe & high, above

the very storm that, only flashing moments

ago, we'd been huddling in for warmth.

Melted at last, liquefied, we became

losers to the blues & victors, both.

Now that he'd blown us away with his shout,

this reigning brownskinned wizard, wise

to the ways of alchemy, squeezed new life

back into us by breathing through cracks

in our broken hearts; coaxing & choking

while speaking in tongues that fork & bend

like the watery peripheries of time; a

crime no more punishable than what the

dreaming volcano does waking from what it was.

Believe me, the blues can be volatile too,

but the blues don't bruise; they only renew.

Squirrels

TRACK 22

Squirrels are skittering
outside thru the trees
of my bedroom window,
laying it on the line
of my consciousness

Brown & black, flurry &
scurrying, how can I not
help loving them like
an old bopster loves licks
laid down building up
so many beats to the moment?

Squirrels may be crazy
but they aren't dullards
They like to play too
They can't be hustling nuts &
hoard all the time. Like
everybody else they love
a good chase now & again

Swishing thru branch leaves,
drumming on my diamond roof,
the shining young squirrels
are making & saving the day

A Little Poem About Jazz

for Miles Davis

Sometimes at the beginning of a movie
when they're flashing the title and heavy
credits over aerial shots of old New York—
skyscrapers that aren't really skyscrapers
because you'd have to be miles high to
see them that way on an everyday basis—
I think about *Green Dolphin Street* blown
over with wind and sound, and I picture
Elizabeth Goudge, whatever she looked like,
up on the stand with you, Trane and Cannonball,
a flower in her hair, a song in her throat.

Dark Red

In an atmosphere of jungle fever,
you wait for Jane to say it again:
"Yes, Father, but what you forget
is Tarzan is white — like us."
Therein lies the rub-a-dub-dub
that pins our eyes and ears to the Ape Man
from here to eternity all out across
the Snows of Kilimanjaro. Poetry,
the dark, red color of blood, courses
through our veins the way Tarzan's call
arrests us as children of the diaspora.
From here we go to places no one planned.
Radio Pictures, Republic Pictures, RKO,
MGM, Warner Bros., Paramount, 20th
Century Fox—all of them worked
the dark side of all streets. Slave trader and
Nazi Errol Flynn made *Robin Hood*.

With Olivia de Havilland his heroine, Flynn flew
back to 1191, the days of Richard the Lion
Hearted and the Crusades, Norman stuff:
barons and fiefdoms and all the land-
grabbing and slave-making pageantry
soon celebrated as empire; colonial, baronial.
To paraphrase New York's Al Smith:
No matter how elegant the script,
it's still baloney. The insolence of history
penned by missionary revisionists,
the awkward thought of Britain now—
O wow. O culture, O buttermilk, O yogurt!
That you were in your lover's arms and she
were fit to last the length of dreams.

Jungle Strut

in memory of Gene Ammons

Of all the nights, yours were greenest, Gene,

bluebreathing son of your boogie-bled dad

who, like you after him, left this dry world

a treasure tray of cocktails for the ear.

You loved making people high with your song

just as you must've loved soaring some yourself.

How high? Moon high, scaling neon heights like

an eagle humming along on silence and a bellyful.

Dumb hunters stalked you, staking you out shame-

lessly, especially when you were straddling air

pockets that, however turbulent, never blew away

your sound and rollicking command of flight.

The wine poured from your jug (when you weren't

locked up in one) was aging and tasty. Bottoms up!

The Art of Benny Carter

There are afternoons in jazz
when a leaf turns and falls
with so much barely noticed purity
that the not so secret meaning of
everything men and women have
tried to do beyond keeping afloat
becomes as clear as ocean air.

The Song Turning Back into Itself 3

Ocean Springs Missippy
you don't know about that
unless you've died in magnolia
tripped across the Gulf

& come alive again
or fallen in the ocean
lapping up light
like the sun digging
into the scruffy palm leaves
fanning the almighty trains
huffing it choo-choo
straight up our street
morning noon & nighttrain
squalling that moan
like a big ass blues man
smoking up the sunset

Consider the little house
of sunken wood
in the dusty street
where my father would
cut his fingers
up to his ankles
in fragrant coils
of lumber shavings
the backyard of nowhere

Consider Nazis & crackers
on the some stage
splitting the bill

Affix it all to
my memory of Ma
& her love of bananas
the light flashing
in & out of our lives
lived 25¢ at a time
when pecans were in season
or the crab & shrimp
was plentiful enough
for the fishermen
to give away for gumbo
for o soft hullo
if you as a woman
had the sun in your voice
the wind over your shoulder
blowing the right way
at just that moment in history

The Song Turning Back into Itself 5

The song skips around
The song jumps
like a little boy
leaps a mud puddle

I park in rainlight
I run out of rhymes
I splash thru the puddle
I land in a change
for 10 years seem like
water be rolling
off my back
one bead at a time
but with light
in the center of
every single one

The song sings new images
variations on the theme
of human love &
its shadow
loneliness
(Billie Holiday
might've been busy
feeding on nuances &
loving a man but
she would've understood,
understanding being
the only honorable escape
in the end)

Sing me shadows
Sing me puddles
Sing me rain
Sing me holidays & nights
Sing me holiness
Sing me loneliness

Sing me a skip & a jump
    across a thousand years

But don't sing love,

    just signal

Tango

You're going to dance with the tiger.
Don't worry, your life is in danger.
Remember your instructions. Listen up.
And suffer, motherfucker, this is the tango."
Enrique Fernández
(from the jacket notes for Astor Piazzolla's Zero Hour*)*

A tango of Mickey Mouses and Argentine wine?
That was their ticket, feckless as flypaper.
Slum lord night, what traps did you drum up for them
in those rose-strewn suburbs where freeways hum
on either side of their slumber, where medicated
mornings spin out of control and tulips turn
into crickets that dance, igniting the negotiable light
of afternoons? Paris could never jolt them now,
nor Buenos Aires or any of those pretty cities
where the tango made its name, where finally
it turned respectable like its off-color cousins—
the waltz, the blues.

                    Loose-hipped, broken-legged,
its accents fleshed out in the wrong places
(in squalid, unwashed bourgeois minds, in lies),
the tango safeguarded many a dangerous evening.
Vehement entertainment, maybe; ballroom rapture, yes.
The tango met them head on, hard, making and gaining
its points, propositioning its sway step by step
at off-hour stops the heart will always make.

By Heart

The leaves on the trees,
the smell of the ocean,
the feel of the earth—
we sit embalmed in lonely clubs
at night, remembering this,
feeling sorry for ourselves
when all the time God is
whispering and zinging
along the telephone wires
of our secret hearts,
telling us, "I love you,"
showing us how. And yet
we shut that soft voice out
like the wind in a leaky cabin.
We know all this by heart
but we forget until the singer
makes the insides of us tremble
like the leaves on the trees,
then suddenly we smell the ocean
and feel the earth whirling
around and around the worlds
of lazy space between our thoughts.

Potato Head Blues

There used to be a happy blue sound that went around
the world and made what passed for a joyful noise—
if not for real, it usually came down to some kind of deal.
Unto the Lord the people submitted mash notes, the ultimate
potato head blues: "In God we trust. All others pay cash."

One Hundred Year-Old Jazz Head Tells All

1/

Locus. Focus. Johnny Hodges, his chest
swollen with rhapsodic pride, explains
why he got it bad and that ain't good.
The energy he's putting out and giving up

122

might not take up 15, 16, 18 long-distance
phonecalls in the midwestern midnight or,
in another vein, from four down to five a.m.
But Rabbit is still alive and all in place.
Locus. Focus.

2/

       We shifting now from the world
of jazz reportage, the tabloidal blahs. We
into the throbbing, swollen truth of it, Rufus.
Gradations, that's what we plunging into.
Plumbing might sound more like it; the ways
trombone players will wah-wah and growl at you
all off-key and on, talking like Rabbit can sing.
We music-makers, we time zappers. We got it
down yet and still we all the time going for it
the way that poet Simon Ortiz always be
going for the rain. We got it, all right, but
got it and getting it—good, bad, moody,
muddied—was that ever the point?

3/

       The real
"Rabbit" Hodges, the brutal Ben Webster of it,

123

simmers down to this: It's kissers, not kisses,
that sometime cause the blues. Just like hugs
can cause your chest to swell. And if, just *if*,
you in your solar night or lunar afternoon
have trouble with this, all you got to do is stand,
sit, lie, or squat. Focus. Be still and know.
Then allow these master explainers to detain you
with as heavy a hit of infinity as you can take.
Locus, I call it. Kissers just can't go it alone.

Darkness, Its Very Hang and Feel

To sit in the dark and write about love—
what could you be talking about?
Cooling, soft shadows, the little town

buried under the city, the woods and trees
or desert before the town emerged,
no margin for error, nothing terrifying,

124

just love rolling off your fingertips—
part one, part two, part-time, partytime, oooh
—big notes, little notes, fattening flats;

shimmering (make that shimmying) sharps.
You know how you talk when love comes down.
The way the world worked back in olden times

you came into this world backwards, came
out of the very blackberry darkness you knew
you'd circle back to, crying again; a place

where light gets farmed. Does quiet light shout,
or does it sigh? Lay you to rest down there
where you can be the sun, where you can actualize.

125

Any Inner City Blues

It would be so easy,
afternoons particularly,
to go take that leap
off the Golden Gate
or run full speed head-on
into the legendary path
of anyone's unpaid-for auto
or shoot up a tablespoon of smack
& lie down in the middle of
the James Lick Memorial Freeway

Or to be modern,
contemporary at least—
give your heart to know
folly & false daring:
race thru the ruins of what was
hip once, pollinating flowerchildren
              at large;
small visible recompense for
a hurt that burns to be eradicated,
not multiplied, like
the head-splitting cancer
that surrounds you

126

The Tenderloin

for Conyus

Crack smokers right here in the streets
and pushers, gangsters, girls with guns
who tell you right up front: "You gonna pay me.
I'll hurt a motherfucker." Daughters and kin—
our sisters these. Grown up San Francisco
pure, right here where sunlight drenches hills
so tenderly that liquor glass still lines streets
and curbs, gutters old Gold Rush thugs hugged.
How can this last? What corporate quirks
work down to shatter and shred such bones
with time's dumb pleasures? Cracked, the faces
of young beauty still stand out; all these aces
down in the hole. Lined up to buy one cigarette
at a time, one slice of bread, one slice baloney,
one drumstick, one wing, they understand
the meaning of a breast—that's gonna cost you.
Plenitude drains into this sickness by the Pacific;
a wave of nods. To touch so much as the beat
of a heart counted off inside a hurried, working
mouth is to re-connect with sorrow and bliss.

127

Brownie Eyes

in tribute to Clifford Brown

The chance you took on going for the high
deep playing gives paid off. No highball pleased;
no coke, no speed, no smack, no reefer. Sky—
from sky back down to earth and back you breezed,
aware of nothing but the joy it took
to coast along, a spirit moving out;
Islamic, cosmic, writing your own book.
You played your heart out, Clifford Brown. Your shout,
a flower blossomed from a thorn, reached clean
across the world. Rahsaan got up and walked,
he said. He had no choice. You had to mean
it, every note you breathed. You tiptoed, stalked
the naked meaning of a song, and then you clothed
and held it. Nothing wasted, nothing loathed.

What Is the Blues?

Far away, I suppose you could say,
where I'm always coming back from.
In any event it's where I want to be
—naked, undressable, inaccessible,
at the tip edge of the vanishing point.

Of course I keep thinking of throwing
in the towel but it isn't wet enough yet.
So, on a dare, I keep splashing around,
ducking down and coming up for air: my
tiny fair share of cool fulfillment.

And to vanish wouldn't be so bad.
Look at the visible, behold it slowly
and closely with unreddened eyes.
Without the stirrings of the heart
swimming in borrowed light, what could
we ever possibly lie down and see?

Billie

Music: a pattern etched into time

I suck on my lemon, I squeeze my lime
into a bright but heady drink, soft
to the tongue, cold to touch, and wait

She who is singing enters my mouth,
a portion at a time: an arm, a leg,
a nipple, an eye, strands of hair—
There! Her song goes down and spins
around the way a toy pinwheel does, as
rosy blue blur, as rainbow, whirling
me through her throaty world and higher
Chug-a-lug enchantress, show me your
etchings. Warm me again now with
the red of your Cleopatric breath

On the Road with Billie

Your heart might have been beating like a hammer,

but this was not a drama I needed, much less staged.

Black and Catholic out of Baltimore. What else?

Who did you think you were? I thought I knew.

The sound of dreams remembered—that's who.

You covered the waterfront. We dogged the road.

There was no way those clouds were going anywhere

without us drifting right along. "No quarrels,

no insults, and all morals"? Hardly. In flooded Oregon

we had to get used to wet and wet and wet, and get

their jokes about web feet, and get it that patches

of blue popped up often and oddly around 4 p.m.,

wake-up time, just outside Portland. God bless

the child who knew you didn't need to drown

your past regrets in coffee and cigarettes, when

we soaked up hours so ripe with rain we learned

every *DETOUR AHEAD* sign by heart. Sex didn't fix.

In this itinerary, the lovesick sound of you worked

more than willows. That trip you took on the train
to get there, remember? "When it rains in here,"
you sang, "it's storming on the sea." Baby, speak
for yourself. You were the one as hard to land
as the Isle de France. Taking a chance on love,
you took a fall. You had your songs to keep you warm.

You wished on the moon. "Some other spring," you
sighed, then slipped through June, a sieve, and got
so high you couldn't get back by the Fourth of July.
The local fuzz, a fan, knowing I'd be freaked,
rang up all sing-song, mocking you, and said:
"That love won't turn the trick to end despair."

Billie, the tricks you turned, the twists blues took.
Why people tear the seams of other folks' dreams
was all it ever was about for you. Am I unfair?
Some kiss did cloud my memory. Still, I smuggled
you to Seattle. At every stop that we made,
I thought about you, too. The crack of dawn

and that crack you peeped through, the one leading
back—was all the crack there was back then.
When the war broke out and opium split town,
up jumped smack, and you and all your hophead
pals went down and copped. "You go to my head,"
you groaned. Where did it all go? Where did you go?

"I get no kick from cocaine"? "Mere alcohol
doesn't thrill me at all"? It made you smile awhile.
The war? They changed the chords, the beat,
you know, it never stopped. They changed the bill.
The War on Poverty, it bombed, but War on Drugs,
it's on a roll, like we were on a roll—April in Paris,

Autumn in New York, Nice Work If You Can Get It;
as if you'd be waiting for me always in the doorways of
Trailways and Greyhounds and train depots, small
hotels with wishing wells, and all the grand hotels;
the same old fine brown frame, sweating like an orchid,
and your heart beat so that you could hardly speak.

Invitation

in memory of Papa Jo Jones
& Philly Joe Jones

There'll be all the requisites
& O how exquisite
the presence of night blooming
jazzmen & women, flowering
in aurora borealis like all the rounded
midnights & Moscow nights & New Delhi
dawns you ever wanted to drop in on
or sit in with or pencil
into your calendar of unscheduled delights.

There'll be love in all its liquid
power, rhythmic & brassy; mellifluous
forms, flashing flesh & the slippery
glittering skin of your teeth;
enchantment, male & female;
the orchid chords of hothouse scat
as pop song, as darkness sweetened
with light; the ascension of steps
that lead to some sumptuous Park

Avenue apartment where a bemoanable lady
lives, sophisticated to a fault, in need
of this bittersweet cultural chocolate,
this quiescent sensation of an invitation.

It'll be big, this gig called life;
the biggest. Johann Sebastian Bach
knew what it was like to bop
through a shower late in the afternoon,
then hang out in your hotel/motel/do-tell
room, wondering what time it really is
back in Iowa City or New Orleans or
the New York of all New Yorks or Rome,
the home you just left the way
autumn leaves—suddenly. Or now it's Paris
where it's going to be wine & cold sandwiches
while you're longing to dine on collard greens
& blackeyed peas with ribs & sauce
hot enough to burn away the sauerkraut &
pig's knuckle of international loneliness.

You'll make your calls & sail off
into an aria or a deep tocatta; in short
you'll honor the invitation your heart
has cabled you direct from the ace,
fulfilling all those requisite licks
so exquisite to the crowd whose deafening roar
will silence all the circus lines
the blue-hearted you never got to deliver.

It'll be the liver of life within who'll know
how *répondez s'il vous plaît* should play.
Just plan to sit & make yourself at home.

A Little More Traveling Music

A country kid in Mississippi I drew water
    from the well
& watched our sun set itself down behind
    the thickets,
hurried from galvanized baths to hear music
over the radio—Colored music, rhythmic & electrifying,
more Black in fact than politics & flit guns.

Mama had a knack for snapping juicy fruit gum
& for keeping track of the generations of chilrens
she had raised, reared & no doubt forwarded,
rising thankfully every half past daybreak
to administer duties the poor must look after
if they're to see their way another day, to eat, to live.

*   *   *

137

I lived & upnorth in cities sweltered & froze,
 got jammed up & trafficked
in everybody's sun going down but took up with the
 moon
As I lit about getting it all down up there
 Where couldn't nobody knock it out.

Picking up slowly on the gists of melodies, most noises
 softened
I went on to school & to college too, woke up cold
& went my way finally, classless, reading all poems,
 some books & listening to heartbeats.

Well on my way to committing to memory the ABC
 reality,
I still couldn't forget all that motherly music,
those unwatered songs of my babe-in-the-wood days
until, committed to the power of the human voice,
I turned to poetry & to singing by choice,
reading everyone always & listening, listening for a
 silence deep enough
to make out the sound of my own background music.

Silent Parrot Blues

"Environmental racism forces people of color, in the words of Rev. Ben Chavis Jr., 'to bear the brunt of the nation's pollution problem.' Examples of environmental racism abound. Called by some 'human sacrifice zones,' these are areas where mining occurs, where pesticide use is rampant, and of course where the pollution of the military, the biggest source of pollution on earth, accumulates and is stored."
Myrla Baldonado, Statement Coordinator:
People's Task Force for Base Clean Up [in the Philippines] *

Even I, who knew next to nothing about parrots, understood that this parrot was exceptional. He didn't curse, he didn't sing; he didn't even speak. Nor did he look well. His coat of many colors was listless and raggedy. Not only did he look as though he'd been plucked and picked on; he looked as though he had been "'buked and scorned," as the faithful Negro spiritual would have it. This sad-faced, underground parrot looked as if he had just been sprung from solitary confinement. And so he had. My mouth fell open when Valve, the parrot's owner, told me the story.

"He's from South America," Valve said, "from Bolivia."

"What kind of parrot is it?"

"A macaw."

"And where do you keep it?" I asked.

"I keep him in there." Valve pointed to the opened door at the end

*Reverend Ben Chavis, Jr., former Executive Director of the NAACP, coined the term "environmental racism." He is a founding leader of the environmental justice movement.

of a row of washing machines that led into a grim and usually padlocked supply closet.

"But," I sputtered, "there are no windows. You mean, you keep him locked up in there in the dark?"

"Look," Valve said, "there's air he can breathe, and what does he need with light? There's really nothing in there to see, is there?"

"But why do you keep him at all?"
Valve turned on his one good leg and said, "Do you know what this bird is worth? He'll fetch me five thousand dollars if he'll fetch a nickel."

"Wow, that's pretty good money."

"Damn right, it is. So now do you understand?"

"No," I told him, "I still think it's cruel to keep any bird locked up in a room with no air and no light."

Indignant, Valve said, "Well, that's your problem. He's going right back in the supply room. I feed him, I give him water. That's all he really needs."

"You got a name for him?"

"Nope, not yet. I bought him off a guy who brought her from South America. You're a writer. You got any good ideas for names?"

Again I stared at the poor creature whose straight-ahead gaze was as stark and as fixed as some of the broken inmates I'd met during visits to prisons, where I sometimes get invited to teach or talk about poetry or storytelling, or to lead workshops. Because my things were almost ready to come out of the dryer, I decided to stay there in the laundry room and read. Shaking my head, I watched in silence as Valve placed clean newspaper, the local tabloid, around the bottom of the cage. For a moment it occurred to me to write a letter to *The Daily*.

*   *   *   *

When I stepped off the elevator, my arms piled high with warm, folded clothes, sheets and towels, there stood Briscoe, my hallway neighbor. An intellectually curious veteran of the American War in Vietnam, Briscoe, a fellow Mississippian, was carrying *The Sirius Mystery* by Robert K.G. Temple, the out of print book he'd recently loaned me about the Dogon people of Mali, West Africa. We shared an admiration for the Dogon. Secretive about their religion, these people know as much and more than contemporary astronomers and astro-physicists about the virtually invisible star Sirius B, companion star to Sirius. Their knowledge of Sirius B predates its modern discovery in 1970 by at least 3200 years. From ancient times, the Dogon have claimed this star as their ancestral homeland. They also knew about Saturn's rings and Jupiter's four major moons millennia before Galileo invented his telescope. Briscoe and I shared an interest in at least a dozen such subjects. We had a rapport.

"You look upset," he said.

"I am upset."

"What about?"

"Just now, downstairs in the laundry room—"

"What happened, man?"

"Valve had a bird, a parrot. And he keeps him locked up in—you know that little room off the laundry room where they keep supplies?"

"The one that's always got the padlock on it?"

"That's the one."

"Wait," said Roscoe. "You're telling me Valve's got some kinda bird locked up in there?"

141

"Not just any bird, Briscoe. It's a fancy parrot from Bolivia. It looked awful. I mean, he had feathers missing and you could tell he wasn't doing so hot."

"Damn!" Briscoe's face lit up. "And it's probably illegal."

"Illegal?" I said, "What it is, is inhumane."

"Inhumane like a motherfucker," said Briscoe. "But why does that surprise you? Somewhere down the line, there's probably some money in it for Valve. I just wish I could get him to come down here and fix my stove."

"And there's stuff I need repaired, too."

"Tell you what you need to do," said Briscoe. "Look, man. You are articulate, and people around here respect you as a writer."

"You flatter me, Briscoe. Do you really think people in Silicon Valley still read anything except tech manuals and how-to books?"

"No, here's what I'm saying . . . You need to write this up and take it over to City Hall."

"City Hall?"

"Take it straight to the mayor and to the city council."

"Briscoe, what good is that gonna do?"

"Al, you know as well as I do—white people don't like that shit. They hate it—mistreating birds and animals, messing over whales and owls and eagles. They won't stand for it. They care more about a missing cat or a dog than they care about you or me. In fact, they're prepared to make your ass extinct in a minute before they'll let anybody fuck with a timber wolf."

"So you're saying—"

"Blow Valve out of the water—that's what. Expose his tacky, cold-blooded ass."

Stunned for the moment at Briscoe's suggestion, I let it roll around in my head until it made me laugh. I laughed so hard I almost dropped my clean laundry.

"That's some funny shit, ain't it?" Briscoe boomed. "Now, they came over here, wiped out the Indians, chopped down the forest, dumped everything they could think of into the rivers and the lakes, buried radioactive shit in places we still to this day don't know about. They got rid of public transportation and put everybody in cars. They got me all messed up with this Agent Orange, tore up those people's country with chemicals and land mines, and now here they come, talking about 'Save the planet.' Sheee-it, the black male—we're an endangered species, too, you know."

"Hey, Briscoe, I'll have to think about your City Hall idea."

"You tell the City what you just now told me. Before you know it, I guarantee, they'll have some kinda special animal rescue squad over here to handcuff Valve and haul him away, and then some organization will up and nurse that parrot back to health."

"Yeah," I said, "if only that parrot would speak up."

*   *   *   *

The incident inspired me to do some reflecting. Early in the last century, and the century before that, most Americans—my grandparents, for example—who knew anything about nature, knew it through work. They hunted and trapped or fished for food; they farmed and preserved. I am now old enough to remember the Mississippi woods and farmlands I roamed and explored with other kids in the 1940s; the creeks we swam, the mineral springs and wells we drank from, and all the farm procedures. We milked cows, churned our own butter, made our own soap, planted and harvested, and picked fruit from trees. We literally lived off the land. Growing up that way, without running water or electricity, using mules and horses for transportation and plowing, we might as well have inhabited the 19th, 18th, or 17th centuries. Agribusiness might have been going strong in California, but it hadn't yet run small farmers off the land in the South.

By the late 20th century, Americans experienced nature largely through recreation: hiking, skiing, surfing, scuba diving, mountain climbing. And yet few realize that it was colonialism in general (and British colonialism in particular) that popularized the notion that nature was something to be tamed or conquered. "The Conquest of Everest," "The Conquest of Space"—such phrases still express relatively recent attitudes towards the natural world.

The capitalist view of nature as an endless source of raw materials and material riches persists. We now know that the present rate of runaway manufacturing and consumption will exhaust and shut down the rain forest in less than 50 years. Does it matter? Does it matter that the crack in the ozone layer, reported some years ago, has grown into a hole the diameter of several midwestern states? One of my buddies now quips that once Americans tire of sports utility vehicles, they'll start driving buses. They'll start passing bills to widen the streets and driveways to expand parking space.

"Can you picture it?" he says. "One or two people to a bus—their own individual, private, personal bus—hogging up traffic and talking on a satellite phone? Or maybe, by then, they'll be looking at their talkmate on a videophone."

In the middle of Europe's 18th century, when romanticism—an artistic sentiment, a predisposition—grew legs and developed as a full-fledged, walking, talking art movement, it traveled quickly to the colonies. Jean-Jacques Rousseau, coiner of the phrase "noble savage," had kicked off romanticism in

France. The individual was It, and not only It, but all that mattered. Literary life alone in England and America thickened with romantic spirit. Rejecting city life and the spread of industrialism, the English romantics—Shelley, Byron, Keats, Thomas Gray, Samuel Coleridge, and William Blake, among others—did their part to exoticize nature.

Nature, in the romantic scheme of things, stood apart from man; romantics viewed it as some kind of "objective reality." Traditional societies, on the other hand, have always regarded man as an inseparable part of the natural world. In America, the prose of Ralph Waldo Emerson and Henry David Thoreau (who, the whole time he was over in Walden, getting close to Nature, brought his dirty laundry home for his mother to do), Nathaniel Hawthorne, James Fennimore Cooper's "noble savage" redskins, Washington Irving, and the poetry of Edgar Allan Poe and Walt Whitman came down hard on the side of romanticism.

In what we like to think of as the post-modern world, romanticism—with its obsessive focus on the individual—is alive and thriving. All you have to do is pick up a mass market magazine, snap on the TV or radio, or surf the Internet to see how deeply we remain under its spell. Advertisements are all about my dandruff, my running shoes, my personal computer, my thirst, my 4-wheel drive Jeep. How would an audience react to a shot that slowly pulls back from a tight close-up on a glamorous model to gradually reveal everything that has gone into the making and disposal of a given product? If in some way we were forced to visualize all the people (workers and marketers), all the fuel (and I would not overlook human nourishment) all the vehicles, all the raw materials, and all the natural resources (including sunlight, rain and wind). When you add to this the decades it has taken to produce the raw materials, and the generations of human beings it has taken to produce all of the people whose brain, muscle, and blood have gone into manufacturing this product, then we've journeyed from a picture to the picture. Connectedness or inter-connectedness is what I'm talking about here.

Vietnamese Buddhist Thich Nhat Hanh includes in his list of The Five Aggregates the idea of inter-origination, which he terms "the interdependence of all events." This couldn't have happened if that hadn't happened. It sounded like heady stuff until I pulled back and started noticing how intimately I was hooked up to everything around me. With everything I could see, feel, touch, smell, taste, remember, imagine, or make up, I was connected and involved. Often the connections were shocking or hilarious. It helped me understand at a grownup level why my grandmother would shift from calm to fury whenever she saw me or any of her other grandchildren fouling the slop pail of food scraps we saved to feed the hogs. You didn't fool around with chicken feed or well water, either. Everyday she and the other oldsters found some reason to tell us: "What goes around, comes around."

*   *   *   *

What connects me to Valve and that sad macaw he was sequestering? Several months after I first saw him with the bird, Valve was fired as building super-intendent. Natasha, another tenant, who was as outraged as I was about the silent parrot, reported to me that the poor bird died in that supply room closet. One day I went down to do laundry and found a large green feather with streaks of yellow, blue, and coral in it

When I showed Briscoe my keepsake, he said, "Ain't that a bitch? You know, man. We got to learn to be more like the American Indian."

"How so?"

"The Indian, you know, knows all about the Great Spirit. The Indian knows we are one with the earth. Shit, our people back in Mississippi knew that, too. If all you got to believe in is this white man's stuff, I feel sorry for your ass."

"But, Briscoe," I said, knowing I would get his goat. "I thought you were a good Democrat."

"Uh-uh, look out now! You know I don't play that Democrat-Republican shit. I figured that one out while I was over in Vietnam."

"Figured what out?"

"It was the Republicans and the Democrats, both, had my ass over there. And it's the Democrats and the Republicans that's got me messed up now. And on top of that, the government still won't admit they did anything wrong. At least we get a little medical attention now. The poor Persian Gulf Syndrome vets don't get shit. It's like my boy John Oliver Killens was saying when he wrote that novel—what's the title of that book we were talking about?"

"And Then We Heard the Thunder?" I said.

"That's it, yes! *And Then We Heard the Thunder.* Man, that's a bad book. I loved it. I'm talking about pure-dee bi-partisan ignorance. Multi-partisan, where that shit be coming at you from all sides. I used to read that book in Vietnam, and then I'd lie down on the ground to catch a nap. I used to get in some good naps over there. But then one of those damn grenades or explosions would go off and wake you up." This was the very way Briscoe and I conversed—that is, on his good days.

"Native peoples believed the earth was alive," I said.

"That's right," said Briscoe.

"The earth was alive, the river was alive, trees were alive, the sky was alive, fire was alive . . . "

147

"Amen, brother."

"And the earth was sacred. The earth didn't leave off over here, then human beings picked up and began someplace else. They believed we were a part of the whole picture."

"That's right," said Briscoe, "but you know you're preaching to the choir, don't you? The earth knew how to take seeds and make 'em grow into whatever that seed was intended to become. Now you got the man fucking with the seeds and fucking with the earth and fucking with the water and fucking with the air and—"

"Hold on, Briscoe. The original meaning of the word 'fuck' is 'to plow.'"

"Oh, yeah? Is that Greek or Latin or something?"

"No, Anglo-Saxon."

Briscoe considered this. "Well, some kinda way, that figures, too, doesn't it? Because they have really fucked over everything and everybody."

"So," I said, "if you believe the earth is alive, and the waters, and the trees and the sky, and you're related to it all—then you treat all of it with respect."

"The Indians did," said Briscoe. "And the Africans did, too."

"But if you don't believe those things are alive, and if you don't believe they have anything to do with you—"

"Except," Briscoe broke in and said, "except provide you with the means to turn a quick buck, like your boy Valve with that pitiful-ass parrot he's got holed up down there . . . "

"In which case," I said, picking up where I imagined he'd trailed off, "it's OK to dump pesticides and nuclear waste and PCPs and anything at all into the earth."

"Right," said Briscoe. "Dump it round where black people and Mexicans and Indians live."

"And poor whites," I added.

"Thank you, brother. You know, Little Charlie—Bubba, like they call him down home—he's so busy believing that bad propaganda they put out about us—hogging up all the welfare, dealing all the drugs, taking all the drugs, committing all the crimes—until he forgets they're messing him over, too. Now, you take Valve with his raggedy self . . . "

"Wait," I said. "I want to come back to something you said."

Briscoe threw up his hands. "Both of us have said so much, I can't remember half of what I just now said."

I said, "But I do. You were talking about ignorance."

"Ignorance, yeah, it's plenty of that everywhere you go. Even right here in Silicon Valley. You ought to hear some of the ignorant stuff I have to listen to when I go out on these computer-programming jobs."

"Well," I said, "to clean silicon requires some heavy chemical solutions, you know. Here in the Valley they send up hundreds of tons of chemicals everyday. People think it's a clean industry, but that's only because they can't see what's happening."

Briscoe, a habitual sniffler, was always trying out holistic treatments for his drastic sinus condition, which was Agent Orange-related. He said, "You don't have to tell me. I'm walking proof. That shit is doing a number on me, on you, on all of us."

"So, Briscoe, tell me, what do we do about all this?"

"I already told you. But since you didn't go down to City Hall, and since you didn't write no letter to the editor of the paper, you still got to tell this story. It takes somebody like you to tell this so people can understand. The average person can't understand what these Green Peace people and ecology people are driving at. I used to didn't understand it, either. Far as I was concerned, that was white yuppie stuff, part of all them protests I missed out on in the sixties and early seventies because I was over there fighting communism, making the world safe for democracy."

Briscoe grinned his sly, coy grin. "At least that's what they told me I was doing. And now China and the United States are tighter than Dick's hat band. Tell you, after this Agent Orange started kicking my ass, I woke up in a hurry. You got to write about this, man. And when you do, be sure and put in there about how crack and heroin, which the CIA put on us, how that's a hazardous waste substance, too. "And put in about all this plastic the government lets big companies package stuff in, then we're the ones supposed to figure out how to recycle it. And get in something about the way they're locking up all the black people and Mexicans in jail, and making it a cheap labor source, business you can invest in on the stock market—work some of that in, too."

I brought the parrot feather upstairs to my kitchen, where I attached it to the hanging wire storage basket of onions and apples and oranges and bananas. I didn't want to forget what had happened.

Remembering the pens people used to fashion from feathers, and that big captive bird's last frozen gaze, I knew I would one day follow Briscoe's suggestion, and get some of it down in black and white.

The Real Bird World

The minute she said it,
  that sharp little girl,
that I couldn't make it
  in the real bird world;

the instant the words
  flew out of her mouth,
Florida came to me,
  anyplace south—

Phoenix, Los Angeles,
  Cuba, Peru
("Nah," said some other voice,
  "Cuba won't do").

On the Peninsula,
  here by the Bay,
pigeons and seagulls
  keep out of my way.

They stay out of my way,
  I stay out of theirs,
but there's just no escaping
  dumb comments and stares

that people throw at me;
  the least of my needs.
The bullshit I've fathomed
  —at high and low speeds!

The household I lived in
  didn't know when to quit—
the TV, the boombox,
  the hours they'd sit

talking crap on the cordless,
  or printing out stuff.
The chitchat, the racket!
  Too much was enough.

So how crazy were they?
  Well, that's hard to gauge.
Not one of them thought about
  me in that cage.

Last week they unlocked it,
  their pager went "Beep!"
I cleared the Dutch door
  without making a peep.

I may not last out here.
  You know how it is.
But I did have the sense
  to get out of showbiz.

Depression, Blues, Flamenco, Wine, Despair

Depression, blues, flamenco, wine, despair—
sunk in, they make you cross your heart and die
for hope. Dark times come at you; they don't care.
"So deal with this," they say. And so you buy
the pain and stress, the restlessness—the works:
low back pain, aches and limps, the twitch
of fear your face betrays.

John "Dizzy" Birks
Gillespie's cheeks puffed out (fat love an itch
scratched by the trumpet at his goateed lip),
they said: "Take chances, stretch, jump at the sun.
You just can't spend your whole life acting hip.
Be corny sometimes. Have yourself some fun.
You can't be cool forever, so relax."

Diz knew puffed cheeks were anything but chic,
but when you closed your eyes you heard him axe
infinitives, split atoms, hairs. You speak
that tongue—curves, flatlands, all of it. You do.

You understand the hoodoo stab of hurt;
the blues, their messy messages, a few
trashed hopes, some lame goodbyes, her skirt,
your coat, the folded jeans, wet tights. Black night
is falling all around you in the rain.
Dark times, dark times can fix you in the light
of reason, recognition, lasers, pain.

Topsy: Part 2

How overwhelming

that Lester tune

heard just out of the rain

early one night

in a café bar

full of African students

midtown Madrid

September 1963

young & dumb & lonesome

a long ways from home

amazed at my tall

cheap rum & coke

patting the wetness

from my leathered foot

to that Lester tune

cut by Cozy Cole

blown from a jukebox

right up the street from where

Quixote's Cervantes once died

Disco Revisited

Disco did and disco didn't—it was as simple as that.
Don't let them blame all those white suits and big collars
and cocaine twisted up into $20 bills on you, disco.
Remember how you used to watch the sun go down?
Every stopped clock flashed shiny sweat orgasmic
all hauled to the beat radio deejays lucked up on.
Filing records by tempo, it was deejays who came up
with so many beats per minute, a formula.

There was always a Seventies lick that laughed it up
with snorts and strobe lights and long grooves;
a twinkle, a primal ritual a mating dance and leftover,
underlying old-school group gropes from the Sixties.

You even got to show your feathers for a long ten minutes
while everybody checked you out so they could check you in
and out and inside-out an all over and underneath
you could check the sun going down in a beer glass

Every stopped clock flashed shiny sweat; orgasmic.

Over the delayed din-as-now trill of track overlays,

music got composed, assembled, timed, packaged, shrunk

and rushed into the Rx Disco, where disco did and

disco didn't relieve the wound-blue pain of staying alive.

Your Basic Black Poet

He mounts the stand &
people turn colors

Where in the world
could he be coming from?

What can he tell us new
about the racial situation?

Why are there oceans in
his poems, sunshine, glacial
journeys toward reunion?

What's the matter with
his diction man he
sho don't sound that black?

Now if he was from Johannesburg,
better yet from Mozambique
or even from St. Martin's
it would be easier to relate
all them drumbeats & bananas
in his blood with the sun
pounding down & around,
that Afric look a sound.

Anyway if he was for real
he'd be off chasing flies
way out in left field or
recovering a broken jaw
from a bigtime heavyweight bout,
off into Ghanaian ghettoes,
revolution rapped in a gown.

Any way you look at it
the dude is irrelevant,
& dangerous to the community.

Herrick Hospital, Fifth Floor

for a musician friend who
finally OD'd on Blackness

Well, so you've gone & overdone it again,
overdosed yourself this time on Blackness;
locked between Blue Cross, nurse-padded walls,
the unreliable air outside & beyond
shot up with softening Berkeley sunshine

Phrasing fails you, diction cramps,
are a loss & reflection too costly
What color were you ever but infamous blue?

If music weren't sound & its realness
didn't cleanse, I know you could never walk
much less dance out of this white room again

Blues for Malcolm X

When I decided to go hear you speak
that week, it was Oakland, it was way out
west, it was long before Blue Tooth tech,
it was youth, way back before truth
got put on commission. I was older
than the early Sixties, younger than rain.

It was when a café colleague declined
my invitation for her to join me to catch you
that I got it right. She was white.
She declined. She declared: "No, you go.
I don't think he'll like me very much."
My political black friends—none of them
had the time, either. I took the bus.

To bust the chops of integrationists—
your mission exactly. You carried it out
with charisma and charm. For dignity

and equality you spoke. "I love all black,

brown, red and yellow people," you said

at the close of your spellbinding talk.

Then you blew us kisses. This is memory.

Now the very government that shot you

down for dead has made you postage,

stampable, sendable, official at last.

Does this surprise you? Official history

—a snake that hisses, a snake that hushes—

smoothes you out, burnishes. I still prefer

the kids who called you Malcolm Ten.

They didn't know where to hide you, so

they put you on a stamp. With Booker T.,

who wouldn't sit with Woodrow Wilson

and the First Lady at his White House Dinner,

you wanted us to separate and split.

And that was it: You, Malcolm X, would fix

the system with the ballot or the bullet.

May these blues clarify your red position.

The John Coltrane Dance

Fly on into my poem
Mr Love Trane—

I know the air isn't all that green
but the sound the sound
the sound above all else
hovering there
vibrating my chair
making the tree dance
the sunrise astound,
the sound surrounds us

—the Alabama surge,
Little Rock,
Philadelphia P.A.
(where that sound must have smoothed stones
& cleansed the veins of many a Quaker);

hurt song,
the tag-along

(I know sound cures)

162

In this fickle sea
of sound
that churns in waves
on all the sides of my becoming,
let the song be you,
Mr Love Trane—

In this long day of spirit
let song be night
& the showering of notes
stars in that beloved firmament

The Lovesong of O.O. Gabugah

Time to split now, you & me
got things to do, got stuff to see,
like Frankenstein breakin loose from his slab
all charged up with juice & ready to swoop
right out the front door & down the stoop

163

past alleyways & neon signs
& people waitin in movie lines:
runs that lead like a big commotion
for all we know into the ocean
where they keep tellin us all life was born . . .
Hey, don't stand there goin, "What's happenin, Gus?"
Let's split before they start zappin us.
Up the street the girls & bitches brew
scuttlebutt about J.R. & Donahue.

The snowy line that blows its way up $100 bills,
the snowy freeze that jacks its frost off $100 bills
cornered all its licks into one big evening of tongue,
went crazy tryin to figure out its next move,
whooshed up the chimney clean, burnt out a nose,
& sniffin all there was to know about July,
just blew its ownself out, forget the rose.

Extraordinary Rendition Blues

I bust into your house, your flat;
I shoot your dog, I drown your cat.
You haven't done a thing to me,
but in my mind I clearly see
when and how you might go to acting
crazy, so I get busy manufacturing
reasons why I had to attack. Meanwhile
I smack you upside the head and kill
your mama, your sister, your neighbors
dead. Yet and still, for all my labors,
you haven't done what I said you did.

I am Big Daddy, you're just some kid.
How many ways I can bust your chops?
At New York, Chicago, all points, all stops
I pick you up and ship you to Syria,
Egypt, Romania, anyplace inferior
to where I'm coming from—the Free World,
man. We'll rescue all you women yet, girl.
We'll wipe terror areas clean off the map.

But they will wire your genitals, let you nap
to heavy metal turned up all loud.
"Hey," you tell me, "three's a crowd!"
Please quit screaming you didn't do
anything to me. It's a little bit too
late for you to be telling me this. Tell it
to Pakistan. No court, global or appellate,
is ever going to hear your story, much less
side with you, alien scum. Confess!
I quote John Wayne: No Pain, No Gain.
Remember that movie? Me Tarzan, you Jane?
Not only will they draw your blood,
my women'll squat over you and flood
your face menstrual red. We study this stuff.
My PhDs will call your bluff.

Myself When I Am Real

for Charles Mingus

The sun is shining in my backdoor
right now.
        I picture myself thru jewels
the outer brittleness gone as I
fold within always.   Melting.

Love of life is love of God
sustaining all life,
              sustaining me
when wrong or un-self-righteous
in drunkenness & in peace.
              He who loves me
is me. I shall return to Him always,
my heart is rain, my brain earth,
my heart is rain, my brain earth,
but there is only one sun & forever
it shines forth one endless poem
of which my ranting, my whole life

is but breath.
        I long to fade back
into this door of sun forever

167

You Do All This for Love

You make me cry. You do all this for love.
You do it all because you dare to care,
you dare to dream. Someone has to act.
You get sick of hearing about how somewhere
over the rainbow. You know too well why

the caged bird sings, but what about the blues
she sings? What about half-notes,
whole-notes, notes in-between? What about
the slot between got-and got-not? Someone's
got to fill that out, indeed, sweet queen of need.

I can stand here all day and tell you how much
I honor, admire, how brave you are. I can
call you courageous, make you a media star.
The truth is this: your kiss to us who survive
in sweatshops, sieves or suburbs, lingers. Amazing,

your courage feels big and tight and warm enough
for me to ask: What will it take to make
more of us feel the thrilling seal of giving?"
To give gets what we need and share. To get
and give back nothing? How incredible, how sad

this wanting world, where women, our deliverers,
get wasted or waste away. Honored, humbled,
I know why you do it, know why I cry and get it
finally that you stun and give more than desert or river.
Recover, discover, deliver—for love you do all this.

The Buddhist Way Out West Reflects on Boots

TRACK 23

The loveliness of poems is that they keep;
the loveliness of lives is that they don't.
The rising tide one-ups the tide that falls
—almost.

         You come to me in nothing
but boots and body-mind. Here blue matches
everything you wear or even think
in this improvised December of cold feet;
a wrinkling cold, twice-iced; now tough as lust.
Your soulful earrings' blue goes smoothly with
the blurred blue of our clouded afternight.

Up one-way streets desire has sniffed us down,
and wired us to this alternating force
for keeps. And yet who knows what anguished tide
will swoop tomorrow up and take us out?

So quickly even poetry (our tree-root deep identity)
can't ride time's wave unthrown. The mystery of love
can't hide for long, either. Come melt my night.

Forget today. Let tides and lives be on
their drunken way. Peel off your sea- and sky-
dyed duds; unstrap your blues and stay awhile.
But don't you, don't you, don't you touch them boots!

Doo-Wop: The Moves

TRACK 24

Let's make no bones about it—whatever
this means or ever meant to you. Darling,
you know your way through what I'm about
to say. Doo-wop still steals the moment,
this sizzling thrill of closeness; the slowness
of our touch too much, too messy to process.

Back when dawn rose off the river, we'd feel it.
Feel felt like enough when flowering was new
and not easy to handle. Neither was breathing.
All that light funneling in from Canada, ferried
over the river while you put a move on my heart.

Heart and soul, flesh and bone—doo-wop
was known to sabotage. All across the land
White Citizens Councils shouted and warned:
Negro music is corrupting White youth. Boycott
Negro Music. We were young, too. You pressed
your hand behind my neck, you kissed my mouth.

Wham! So who'd kissed whom? You still wonder?
In one slow move you slithered and drizzled
snail trails all up and down eroded maps of me.
Doo-wop, stone-slow of step, sticks to you, lasts.

The doo-wop mind cries: O baby you know
I love you, always thinking of you, I place no one
above you, and you know I'll never snub you.
Under doo-wop's spell, you make no bones.
You shake your perfumed boodie. You go for keeps.

Now's the Time

for Gordon Lapides

7:47 a.m.
Charles Parker's message from 1946
or whenever it was teaches us

that beautiful eternities dwell inside moments
& reverberating forever
charge us with godliness of creation,
creating by the moment,
ignorance of which
brings us to dead end
upon dead end. I am not anything less
than soul shedding layer after layer
of no-soul that soul may reveal itself
to itself so to speak,
an unvicious actually joyous
circle of commitment & revelation ensues

but you got to get in that groove,
you got to take chances &
avoid romances of daydream

which is no-dream really
but imprisonment,
the door closing,
tears crop up
in automatic
misery
vs.
freedom,

atoms becoming atoms
the earth is built
to crumble away
as God smiles
crumbling begins, ends,
the smiling goes on,
you happen,
keep happening.

Place: everywhere
Time: Now—

7:54 a.m.

175

Jazz as Was

Sometimes it's the flagrant accentuation

of bebop & late afternoon loneliness

that devastates; those early night

hours just don't get it, so everything

that happens long past midnight grows

misty with whiskey & other forms

of practiced behavior. The drummer's

got some new white girl on hold who adores him.

The piano player's totally clean but

won't comb her hair, she's hip to the bone.

The bassist is a communist the way

he scribbles off accompaniment like a giant

bear waltzing africally thru bureaucratic

steps. Hey, it's America heard in rhythm

& enormous harmonies the color of October;

swollen & falling, full of seedy surprises

that make your hoary heart speed up

& do double time between the born-again beats.

Jackie McLean: Alto Saxophone

I
am
forced
to realize
that written
he (the horn player)
gets that unmistakably successful
Iron Age sound:
ripe screams
down elevator shafts
in buildings the upper storeys of which
no artist would prize as loft

I say he's a sunbound Bird

descendant

: the prestidigitator

sure enough

producer of metal flowers

for that's what grows simplest

twixt cracks

in the skin

of a concrete world

of alloyed beams

Ah but flaming within is God's pure orchid

whispering its hearty language

in heady fragrances

Listen

&

glisten

in the aggravation-produced joy

uniting jazz children

the world over

1965–1968
Berkeley, Mexico D.F., Detroit, Palo Alto

178

Tribute

TRACK 25

Yes brothers you invented jazz
& now I'm inventing myself
as lean & prone to deviance
as the brilliance of your
musical utterance, a wind
that sweeps again & again
thru my American window
What a life you sent me
running out into expecting
everyone to know at once
just what it was I was
talking or not talking about

The genius of our race
has far from run its course
& if the rhythms & melody
I lay down this long street
to paradise aren't concrete
enough it can only be because

lately I've grown used to taking
a cozier route than that of
my contemporary ancestors

Where you once walked or ran
or railroaded your way thru
I now fly, caressing the sturdy
air with balls of my feet
flapping my arms & zeroing

A Hymn to Her

(Divine Mother)

Like some swollen, swaying samba
under pressure to behave,
you are wild and without number;
neither principle nor wave.

Can your dance subdue its dancers
when we dancers are the song?
Can your slow, half-whispered answers
float us back where we belong?

Everything we long or ache for is
within soothing reach, it seems.
You surround us with your wakefulness;
you astound us in your dreams.

Watsonville After the Quake

On Central Coast radio KTOM blasts

Eddie Rabbitt thru waves of air the sea

surrounds, & all the other country stars

come out (Claude King, Tammy Wynette, Shelley

West) & spread themselves in droplets.

The sacred moisture of their song is skin

to seal a pain that quavers in this ash-blue night

coming on just now like a downcast motel date,

who's warned you from in front that she'll be coming

'round the mountain when she comes.

Whose tents are these? What's with these shot

parking lot & alleyway families peeping around

the raggedy backs of undemolished fronts?

That brownskin kid on a grassy patch along Main,

catching a football & falling with joy

on the run, is his family up from Mazatlán,

up from Baja or Celaya—or edges of eternity?

Network TV didn't do this news up right.

For all their huff & puff & blow-your-house-down,

the mediators of disaster and distress

didn't find this sickly devastation sexy.

Besides, who's going to cry or lose sleep

over a spaced-out, tar-papered, toppled-down town

by the sea, brown now with alien debris?

Old Trane, San Diego

1/

Under the RR Bridge
a silly even fickle sonance
dances & brings us all around
to rounder, sounder ways of hearing
what the heart flowers
in her private midnight-cum-dawn

hours unobserved. Under Capricorn.
Clouds bring us closer to the dark
sweetmeat of our basic yearning.
Crying, the soul snaps again &
again in dancing clusters of jazz
again, jazz again revolved around
the saxophonic night. Hey, it's
the 20th Century in North America
—almost 21. Do you know
where your promises went? Or what
sky is telling us what?
Hug me quickly and tell me what
I've needed for so long to hear.

Trains' whistles blow in one color only
—blue. And there was no bluer bellow
than the one that comforted me at India
& Date Streets, Little Italy, the strangest
hot January since 1906. Back east the 50-degree
below zero trend was taking off, but
in my room at La Pensione, I was running
the ceiling fan & wondering why I hadn't brought
suntan lotion, That blue-black diesel call
poured into my bed, my coffee, my bath, my bags,
my head & all the books I lay there reading;

the cloud-blue sky protecting Little Italy
by day, the Lamplight District nights.
Downtown, the home of homelessness,
in the 99 cents store, a curious young woman,
all brown & tan, Mexico-born, eyed me up & down
& laughed when I talked to her of earthquake skies.
She might've been remembering Mexico City
the year the whole mountainside trembled
and it all caved in.

        But it was my Spanish;
the very word *terremoto*, a little like
Quasimodo—monsters, both—that made her laugh;
that made me world-weary giggly a halfday late.
At 4:31 a.m. my single hotel bed already had
turned into a waterbed, so strong was the song
L.A. was blowing. "Here we go again," I told
San Diego. "Haven't we ridden this freight car
before? Why didn't your horn sound a warning?"

Snowy Morning Blues

in tribute to James P. Johnson
and Langston Hughes

New York, you know, has its New Yorks,
Manhattan her Queens, the Bronx
keepers of the flames with all their names intact.
Now that's a fact. Upside it, though,
you'll put your heart and everything
you know or thought you knew of snow.

When Snowy Morning Blues plays James P. Johnson's
game of catch-me-if-you-can, you can. He could, too.
New York ain't no last word, you know.
Nothing's what it used to be. And you, the you who sees
out past the end of the world, this snow, this wee wind-
fall he fells us with under eaves the way we all fall
under suspicion in detective movies. Blam!
Blame it on the blues, blame in on a blizzard.

Diamonded, grounded in its ice cream crisscross,
snow makes you take to the country again, harmonica in hand,
craving the guitar of a pianistic You-Gotta-Be-Modernistic
genius—you can't get into this. Let snow tell its own story.
Let the blues roll on. Let snow fall right on time this time
blue, blank, blackening the city-within-a-city christened
in Dutch: Harlem, Haarlem,
Haaaarrrrrlem.
Vermeer, beware.

A Sunday Sonnet for My Mother's Mother

for Mrs. Lillian Campbell

Consider her now, glowing, light-worn,
arthritic, crippled in a city backroom
far from the farm where she was born
when King Cotton was still in bloom.

She is as Southern as meat brown pecans,
of fried green tomato, or moon pies.

Gathering now for eight decades, aeons
of volunteered slavery soften her sighs.

Talk about somebody who's been there,
This grand lady has seen, remembers it all
and can tell you about anyone anywhere
in voices as musical as any bird's call.

Loving her, it hurts to hear her say,
"My grandchildren, they just threw me away."

Springtime in the Rockies

Alive in the circumference of this moment, and bubbled
here, buoyed by winds of time, we settle further in
for grander rides than this: an infant Denver afternoon
warmed up by Mozart, Rimsky-Korsakov, the sound
of home that courses through our own blood and thoughts.
That home can only be this slippery minute,
its splash and silence fast upon us—first as rain,
and then again as snow. Embroidered with new clouds,
or lathered with the skin of rain, humidified,
we escape the great indoors to feel out for ourselves
a city pretty enough to risk our lives to reach by jet.
And yet the feel of Denver—the itchy eyes, the froggy throat,
dry nose—it just won't change. Her winos, cowboy hats,
and Indian men and women, brown-bagged, twisted;
her grizzly roughnecks, loan sharks, liquor stores;
and Spanish-speakers (knowing Colorado means
colored, painted-in) reclaim the sun-washed West.
The legendary Buffalo Bill Memorial Museum and Grave
on Lookout Mountain, Molly Brown (unsinkable,
remembered for the gold she and her husband J.J. stashed)—
Victorians. Coors Brewing Company, still tapping
beer from 44 natural springs—icons. Such are the sights

we flock to peep. "Leave them alone," the nursery rhyme
advised, "and they will come back." Like spring to the shores
of rivers loved and kept, love comes back. The West came back.
With majesty the month of March moves in to do again
exactly what it needs to do: surround us with imagined time
dissolved to make almighty mountains, pikes and peaks.
Thus clutched by height, tall light and breathing room,
circumferences, diameters and time, we move, alert, alluvial, alive.

Cold Sweat

James Brown, 1967

"Excuse me while I do the boogaloo!"
Outrageous!

I sat riveted behind the wheel, realizing at last why those pantyhose
packagers had the insight to name their product Sheer Energy.

Sheer energy was what James Brown was pushing; pushing and pulling
and radiating in ultraviolet concentric circles of thermo-radiant funk. It was
sheer energy with a whole lot of soul and blues slipped in—or, rather, thrown
in, the way you might sell someone a 45 rpm disk or a .45 pistol—in this

case, it doesn't matter—and throw in a shiny new Peterbilt truck for good measure, for the hell of it.

I was so carried away by the blues—grounded yet floating, gritty glide of it that I pulled the car I was driving off to some side-street curb, cut the engine, cranked up the radio volume, and just sat there, steaming in the warmth of that afternoon to let myself be swayed and lilted and swooshed by the James Brown sound.

James Brown and the Famous Flames. He had that right, too: the band was on fire. I sat in the car, my limbs going limp, sweat popping out of my forehead, I rolled the windows down in time to catch a lazy, passing breeze. That's when it hit me.

Right then and there, the whole arrangement got etched into my burning brain; I soaked it all up—blowzy blue lines, vine-like rhythm, the works. It happened so fast and took so completely that when I found myself out on a dance floor at a party a few nights later, all I had to do when "Cold Sweat" came on was combine what I'd absorbed with the feeling of the moment. The movements and motions took care of themselves. The trance was complete. I and my partner, we must've been glowing out there with the lights down low.

What was, was hypnosis; hypnosis by osmosis. The hips gyrate; the nose opens. There was nothing subtle about it. I can even remember sitting there in the car, thinking: "They oughtn't be broadcasting this thing to drivers of cars. In fact, they need to slap on of those warning blurbs on the record itself that says: "Under no circumstances is this music to be listened to while driving or operating dangerous machinery!" And, even while we were dancing, working ourselves up into a fever, I kept flashing on those festive occasions in the

Caribbean where, when funk grew too thick or body heat too scalding, all you had to do was dash outside, race down to the seashore, peel off your duds, and rush into the water to cool down.

"Cold Sweat," the first time I heard it, had me swaying so far out there in musical space I was ready to either melt into the upholstery or get out and dance all over the top of the car. And by the time James Brown and the brothers broke into cries of "Give the drummer some!" my sticky, hot hands were already playing the dashboard as though it were a three-piece conga set.

"Funky as you wanna be!"

"Keep it right there!"

"Excuse me while I do the boogaloo!"

Romance without Finance

TRACK 26

If you can't finance it undercover,
you needn't apply for the gig of lover.
To stake this whittled down version of love
you don't need money so much as time,
attention & all the me the mind can see.
Still, moments turn up with dulling precision
when the heads or tails of your nighttime thereness
must be flipped to recall your daytime awayness;
no win, no lose, just edgily the blues.
As money needs spenders & spenders need lenders,
so passionate romance seems always in need
of love, back-talk & deliberated speed.

Easy Overhead

Can working the hot look of lovers and dreams
into what cool clouds might be thinking
of a glittering moment, or a lifetime of wanting
to be happy at the next exit ever easily end?

Imagine the histories of all clouds
in embryo, risen like music
from watery earth spirits heated,
sparked by fire, blown by wind.
Where do they come from,
where do they go?

People say if you've seen one cloud
you know them all. How can that be?
Just smell for yourself these perfumed clouds
hovering at the shadowy end of day
over a floating Paris, a saddening Paris;
a Paris even Helen of Troy would have to call dull.

How delicious the gypsy-like trickle

of Frenchified rain;

south-silenced rain that wets my glistening head;

a food of clouds digesting in my ears.

Just a Flat-Footed London Singer

for Joan Merrill

Jazz, what were you supposed to be?
I'm not that woman at the microphone,
gardenia scented from habits older
than and bolder than time. Time is a thief,
sayeth Kurt Weill, speaking you.

195

How California spoils and spills over
into the simply complex Billie songs
of a lovely Marin County afternoon
emphatically post-London. Lotte Lenya?
Did you hear what just got said

in British to perfectly match your German-
smart American English? Chilly but rarely
foggy these days, London bristles, London
bridges brag, and London walks me home.
I'm not that woman at the mike, but sing

I still can do. "A Foggy Day," no, but
weather—thick and wet, unsilhouetting—
works. Scotland knows; the Irish coast
surely. The London loving me was always
furry with cloud, comforted with it

and smoky in the cigarette permissiveness
of my European unions. Like Etta Jones,
I never was much for shaking my shoulders
to signify this, or raising my eyebrows
to signal that. I'm just a flat-footed London singer.

New Orleans Intermission

A lighted window holds me like
high voltage. I see . . .
Walter Benton,
This Is My Beloved

1

I see it zooming down
over the bayou late April
morning of the brightest green
from the window of a jet named Nancy

Settling back childishly
in the sky all alone,
my secret hand waves light aside
to get a better look at
all the music coiling up
inside me again as I watch
this still virgin landscape

Is that the famous Mississippi
down there, are those the streets

197

Jelly Roll did his marching,
strutting, & poolsharking in?
Was I really just born
a gulf away from here or
carved like Pinocchio
from some thick dark tree below?

2

The only way to love a city's
to live in it till you know
every door every store every
parkingmeter deadlawn alleycat
district smell pussy hotel
gumwrapper & wino by heart

Airborne all night my sleepy heart
leaps like windblown raindrops

I'm a very old baby reentering
an unchanged world with a yawn

3

Yes I've lived here before
just as I know & can feel in my tongue
that I've tramped this earth as
storyteller & unaccountable thief
too many times before,
a displaced lover of spirit & flesh

Riding the St. Charles trolley nights
an old American, classically black,
spots me as a tourist & softly explains
how he don't have to take snapshots
no more since he can more or less
picture in his mind what's keepable

When I take this 15¢ ride, the cool
off-hour breeze tightening my skin,
I can time in to people telling their
stories real slow in the form of asides
& catch myself doing a lot of smiling
to hold back tears

Old-timer tells me
why the fare on this line's so cheap:
"It's so the colored maids & cooks &
gardeners can git to they jobs & back
without it bein a strain on they pocket"

4

On Bourbon Street (North Beach or
Times Square) a fan-tailed redhead in
G-string & nothing else waves me
into a topless/bottomless joint with a
dog-faced barker posted at the door
who yips & howls: "C'mon in yall & see
southron gals takin off they draws
for just the price of a drink!"

It isn't
enough to laugh & rush in like a
prospective drunk in heat

The point is that love & love alone
holds up my feet as they step from
Bourbon to Rampart Street, dreaming of
Congo Square, Creole intrigue, Fats

200

Domino & Dr John while a black panhandler
(cross between Satchmo & Papa John Creach)
hits on me for 50¢ in front of Al Hirt's

5

Steaming hot down in front of us now:
ham biscuit eggs grits Cajun coffee
& a solid glass of buttermilk for me
for fun—

It's Mama's in the morning
where American poet Miller Williams
leans past his dark wife, Jordan, to say:
"You probly the only Californian that
really knows about this place, man"

I know I'll slip back by for gumbo,
for lunch known down here as dinner,
or for a supper of 90¢ crawfish bisque

But right now it's the light quivering
in from the street down onto our plates
that makes us quit talking poetry

"I'd give up writing," Miller sighs,
"if I could sing as good as Ray Charles"

Tomorrow they'll drive back to the Ozarks
Tomorrow I'll fly back to California
where there're no nickel phone calls,
pick up the show from where I left off
& read Marie Laveau the Voodoo Queen

Flirt

Like somebody's ass in a Friday Nite Video,
stop-framed to rock & shock the world
out there looking, the sweet wiggle
of your thought-waves saves me hours
of guessing who's kissing me now.
Lust is just that crazy; a lazy display
of worn-out backseats. *Nowhere to run to . . .*
Nowhere to hide. . . Let's put this on rewind,
pretend the beginning's the end. Let's
pretend you'll let me think you never winked.

Why Love Bach's Goldberg Variations?

Where does it say that armies ennoble a nation, and what of bread,
the spendable and expendable kind? Where do we go when we need
to tear hands off the clock? To the local recruiter? The credit union?

Bank on beauty every time you feel the pull of knowing forces.
Put it any way you wish, but keep that wish alive. Johann Sebastian
Bach knew so intimately the ins and outs of how time worked
its keys and silences at intervals that he could let the whole world go
up in a sacred flame of sound. God, the beautiful changes!

In tender surrender, the soft sound of blues spread out around you
fools you good. Glenn Gould, Keith Jarrett—play the morning
differently. The moment you fall in love you get it. Everything
there is to know about love you grasp, understanding how it can go.

To go godlike, go like the wind, defies the theologian's guess.
Afternoon and evening bloom and nurture you. Note by note
you rise and fall, you speak and listen, whisper, moan and shout
your momentary case, then move on, certain to return renewed.

Going for Broke

To go for broke, in the gospel sense, means
going for the gold, going for good, going for God.
Onlookers sometimes wonder how blues people
or rhythm & blues people or even bad news people
can suddenly do the old-fashioned twist on a dime
and start preaching. Or, like Little Richard, how
can they at the close of a show shout, "I have been saved."
They *have* been saved. Like a document that, up until then,
was still getting written, converts get saved automatically,
and there doesn't have to be a flash of lightning or
a whole lot of shaking or incense going on. To go for broke,
in the gospel sense, means giving up everything you've got
(or thought you had) to God, giving up everything you were
(or thought you were) to the Lord, and giving up everything
you did (or used to do) to Jesus. Once God moves in,
He breaks the house—your flat, your duplex, your studio,
your room—and moves you into one of His many mansions.
Al Green sings, "Take me to the river. Wash me down."
The man once given to the religion of Saturday night
becomes the same one who shakes your glad hand Sunday
morning, and the same Creator who wrote the script
directs and stars in it, too. Sparing no expense. Going for broke.

204

Something About the Blues

"When was the last time you / saw a dog eat a dog? /
When men invented the term / Bitch / they were talking about /
themselves."
—Ishmael Reed

Something about the blues that catches way down in the throat of
Howlin' Wolf or Taj Mahal, that tingled the nipples of Dinah
Washington and Leontyne Price

Something about the blues can drive a good woman mad, make her
give up and take up shopping carts to push the homeless streets
and die without the dignity of a dog

Something about the blues can also cauterize the wound that
wobbles around the winded world like a hula-hoop

Something about the blues swoops down on you so soft and easy
that the slippery salt-seam that sews sleep to wakefulness melts
down to let love pour out all over you like radiation

Something about the blues tunnels through you straight up to the
bottom of all that oils

Something about the blues makes a billionaire tremble when she
knows she stands to lose half a billion

Something about the blues looks back at you, an ancient star
creature, every time you stare into the night sky from a place
uncompromised by urban light-leak

Something about the blues belongs where sound leaves off and
light takes up the spectral hum

Something about the blues would sooner draw blood than breath in
this fragile century that streams out beyond total horror

Something about the blues outlasts the subtle electricities the
science of our time has yet to find, much less map or capture or comprehend

Something about the blues curls around the world like a Yankee-
sized question mark

Something about the blues makes you wonder (if you still wonder,
if you still dream) what's taking Earth under

206

Statement on Poetics

Music—with which poetry remains eternally intimate—seems a dead ringer, as it were, for life itself. And while each also seems invisible, I always catch myself asking: What is life but spirit; spirit-thought made hearable, seeable, smellable, touchable, and delectable?

Who hasn't sung or listened deeply to songs, re-lived recordings, or melted into some performance to the point of identifying almost irretrievably not only with the sound and inner look and feel of music, but with all of its inexplicable beauty; the rapture, the crazy, life-quickening sense of it?

"Man," Jackie McLean told Pacifica Radio's Art Sato in a late 1980s interview, "if we wanna sound like airplanes . . . we can be an airplane, man." McLean was recalling the reluctance of trumpeter Lee ("The Sidewinder") Morgan to parachute into terrain he hadn't even surveyed before, much less explored. With trombonist-composer Grachan Moncur III, they were rehearsing Moncur's modal, eerie-sounding "Air Raid" for the ground-clearing 1960s Blue Note album, Evolution.

"So," McLean is supposed to have said to Morgan, his longtime soul-buddy, "let's be an airplane, you know. 'Cause Grachan is different, man. He likes Frankenstein and Donald Duck and a wide variety of topics, weird topics to write music to."

As Mary Shelley's 1817 horror story and Walt Disney's cartoons have inspired movies, costumes, whole philosophies, and music, so music routinely provides poets with "*a wide variety of topics, weird topics.*"

Like jazz players and all the other artists and poets, I want to fly, to sail, to leap and jump and jaywalk; I want to walk, skate, surf, skateboard or ski across barriers. If I play Gene Ammons' "Canadian Sunset" and Thelonious Monk's "Carolina Moon" back to back, can you imagine how an escaped slave must have felt once she actually reached Toronto or Montreal? How powerfully odd she must have felt to look back at herself, plotting this break; back there outside Raleigh or Charlotte, where the passing thought of Canada was a dream.

I want to zoom forward and at the same time be watching everything rush by me through the porthole blue of some cloud-blown sky-ship. Or, back-lit, seated at the window of a train, Duke Ellington's favorite composing site, I have no trouble seeing and hearing centuries whiz past.

Einstein had it pegged; the mover isn't always necessarily moved by all this movement. Grounded in stillness, rooted in silence, all motion, like sound, feels hopelessly yet deliciously relative. Even so, the beauty of all these scheduled and improvised arrivals and departures neither fades nor reaches any point that even remotely resembles a fully orchestrated stop.

Like the advancing hands of a clock closely watched, the action we know as music or poetry will sometimes appear to stand still. But in truth it is only the quiver and shimmer of being profoundly alive and for-real that slows. The sweet, hot solo jam of believing what you hear just plays and thickens and builds.

After 60 years of listening, I still feel as though I can't get started; as though I have so little to say about jazz and the roles all music continue to play in that curtainless sun-room in the mansion of my life, where thinking and telling take bloom.

Index